Praise for *The Unintentional Comedian*

"Kelli Houston's *The Unintentional Comedian* is a bold, brilliant memoir that pulses with heart, humor, and hard-won wisdom. With disarming honesty, Kelli shares her journey through identity, ambition, and purpose: building programs from the ground up, challenging institutional norms, and rediscovering herself along the way. Her professional accomplishments are extraordinary, but it's her openness that sets this book apart. She writes with the same courage and compassion she brings to real life, inviting readers to reflect, laugh, and heal alongside her. Kelli is one of the most thoughtful, remarkable people I know, and her story is a powerful reminder that real leadership starts with vulnerability. This memoir doesn't just inspire, it changes you."

Meredith Anastasio, JD
Management Executive
www.maevents.info

"Reading *The Unintentional Comedian* feels like being welcomed into the heart of someone who has turned her life's challenges into purpose. Houston writes with bravery, compassion, and authenticity, offering stories that uplift and inspire. A beautiful tribute to justice, love, and the strength of the human spirit."

Sue Orchard, PsyD
Educator

"In this deeply personal and powerful memoir, Kelli takes us on the journey of a lifetime—her own. From coming out as a Black queer woman and navigating the complexities of family, to shaping an ever-evolving career as an equity and inclusion leader and executive, Kelli's story is one of courage, resilience, and growth. With her blend of warmth, wit, and fearless honesty, she reflects on the private and public challenges, career successes, pitfalls, and moments that tested not just her resolve but her identity.

Over the years I have known Kelli, I have been moved by her insight, strength, and unwavering commitment, as well as by her ability to find humor even in life's hardest moments. This is a story of becoming, of rising through the challenge and finding laughter and healing along the way. And most of all, Kelli's is a story of love."

Shawna Unger
DEIB Executive Consultant, Allen & Unger Consulting

"*The Unintentional Comedian* tells Kelli Houston's personal and professional journey with vulnerability and honesty. Her relatable stories offer an authentic look at an equity champion's work and her grief over losing her parents. It's a humorous, gripping, and passionate account by a survivor I am proud to know."

Pleasant Radford Jr.
Health Equity Leader

"Who are we? Why are we here? In *The Unintentional Comedian*, Kelli Houston delves into these timeless questions with humor, wit, and unflinching vulnerability. As our nation grapples with the humanity of healthcare and the consequences of inequitable access, Houston calls on readers to demand systems that are inclusive, compassionate, and just.

At its heart, this memoir is the story of a woman whose courage and resolve never waver. With quiet strength, Kelli faces personal and professional trials, inviting us to walk beside her as she revisits a turbulent childhood, says farewell to a cherished father, and stands up for traumatized children in emergency rooms. We grieve with her, celebrate with her, and ultimately grow with her.

The Unintentional Comedian is a tribute to the power of small acts of kindness and a celebration of a woman who, by standing firmly in her truth, has planted trees whose shade she may never know. My time with Kelli through these pages was moving, memorable, and deeply inspiring. Highly recommended."

Melanie Gloster
Mental Health Advocate

"Kelli is such a spectacular storyteller. From the first word, you can feel the strength, heartbreak, and tension of the beautiful story that is her life. Her ability to make you smile, laugh, and even be on the verge of tears is not accidental—it's the skill that comes only from deeply lived experience and the grit to make out on the other side to share it with us. Imagine sitting next to your best friend at your favorite park bench and losing yourselves into the night with the stories of life. This is the feeling you will have when reading *The Unintentional Comedian*."

Edwin Lindo, JD
Author, Educator, Scholar, Cultural Worker

The Unintentional Comedian

The Unintentional Comedian

Lessons from a Life Unexpected

KELLI HOUSTON

Publish Your Purpose
141 Weston Street, #155
Hartford, CT, 06141

Ordering Information: Quantity sales and special discounts are available on quantity purchases by corporations, associations, and others. For details, contact the author at khouston5057@gmail.com.

Edited by: August Li, Brandi Lai
Cover design by: Nelly Murariu
Typeset by: Medlar Publishing Solutions Pvt Ltd., India

ISBN: 979-8-88797-178-0 (hardcover)
ISBN: 979-8-88797-179-7 (paperback)
ISBN: 979-8-88797-180-3 (ebook)

Library of Congress Control Number: 2025910396

First edition, April 2026.

Publish Your Purpose is a hybrid publisher of nonfiction books. Our mission is to elevate the voices often excluded from traditional publishing. We intentionally seek out authors and storytellers with diverse backgrounds, life experiences, and unique perspectives to publish books that will make an impact in the world. Do you have a book idea you would like us to consider publishing? Please visit PublishYourPurpose.com for more information.

Disclaimer

This book contains adult themes
and discussions of mental health struggles.
Reader discretion is advised.

Dedication

In loving memory of my parents,
Robert and Flora Houston.

Contents

Foreword

It was early 2017, more than a year into my relatively new role as a founder and CEO, and I was struggling to build a business that would have the kind of impact on the world I envisioned. That was the year a celebrated human rights attorney transformed the way I imagined business success and most importantly made a fated introduction: meeting a senior healthcare executive named Kelli Houston.

Kelli and I met up in a famous Portland restaurant a few days later. We instantly connected around our shared passion and skill for designing affirming healthcare programs and services for transgender and nonbinary patients, a population of people who at the time were distressingly misunderstood, stigmatized, and underserved. I was impressed by Kelli's commitment, as it was no easy feat leading this kind of transformation within a faith-based healthcare organization. As our conversations deepened, I began seeing many opportunities for a powerful collaboration.

Eventually we did collaborate. Kelli had a knack for finding opportunities within large systems to anchor the fundamentals of growing a more diverse, equitable, and inclusive organization. She began by creating programs that I like to call "all plays," which means *everyone* within the workforce can see how their contributions help them do their jobs better, strengthening their relationships with their colleagues and resulting in better business outcomes. I share Kelli's commitment to transforming the culture of work through these types of engagements, to amplify only a flavor of her brilliance.

In May 2022, the murder of George Floyd by a policeman placed great demands on both of our time. Kelli's leadership on executive teams opened up new ways we collaborated, challenging organizational leaders to explore how their roles may contribute to oppressive behaviors, while also empowering them to recognize the significant role they could play in undoing these harms. Truly, we were practicing the art of interpersonal peace, and what a gift it was to share it with a group of leaders who could use their power to create more psychological safety and trust for the people they lead.

Our shared commitment in building spaces of belonging at work and in community brought us together in the early years of my business, and what ultimately resulted was a cherished friendship and a powerful colleagueship that unlocked innovative approaches to upending workplace exclusion and othering. It turned out to be a connection that changed my perspective on how professional relationships can evolve into close friendships over space and time, a perspective that has led to placing chosen friendships as one of the most important relationship constructs in my life.

Kelli and I remain connected around our shared desire for true belonging, felt within a global community. A community where belonging is the only option, embracing what the South African Bantu language refers to as *ubuntu*, which means, "I am because of you." It recognizes the interconnectedness between all humans and all life on Earth.

Kelli and I recognize the sobering obstacles to activating our vision for a belonging society, yet I feel an enormous sense of hope because I know how committed leaders like Kelli are to bringing this vision into reality. I have witnessed Kelli encouraging those she leads to continue to envision a world where a true sense of belonging can be achieved and to begin taking action toward bringing that vision into our shared reality. Kelli's leadership, lived experience, and presence are reasons to feel a greater sense of hope.

And I believe this book you're holding will provide exactly that: *hope*. It's the medicine we truly need at this moment, and it comes from a vision of possibility. I often talk about possibility models, presenting a possibility of a life well-lived in the form of a person who shares an identity another holds most dear. Kelli's stories offer such possibilities in these very volatile and uncertain times.

For many readers, perhaps you, Kelli may offer a new possibility for how to move forward in your life. The stories on the following pages are rarely ones you'll see featured in the media, yet they are the very stories that will likely offer a new way of being in the world that may provide a path for you to find your own authentic route. Allow Kelli to serve as your catalyst to design a life unapologetically on your own terms, and perhaps one day you'll pay it forward by being a possibility model to the next generation.

Kelli's journey to find love, acceptance, and belonging offers a source of strength and courage, two leadership traits many of us need in spades to thrive through these times. Allow this book to inspire you to lean into making brave and bold choices that align with the truest expression of who you really are and what you are called to be in this lifetime. In fact, that's exactly why this book exists. By reflecting, perhaps more deeply than you ever thought you could, it challenges you to find where Kelli's stories end and yours begin and to recognize the core emotions she shares through her stories that you can immediately connect to. That is Kelli's magic, to bridge across what could be perceived by some as a canyon of differences but for Kelli is a way of relating, a model to experience *ubuntu* through her stories.

Leading through these complex times isn't easy, nor is it anything like what you've experienced in the past. Instead of collapsing in on your values or complying with actions or directives you know run afoul of your integrity, I challenge you to find your own bridge to connect more deeply to the stories Kelli shares in her book. If you find yourself in a formal community or organizational leadership position, *you*, in particular, have an obligation to do so.

I lead an organization that's on a mission to upend the epidemic of workplace exclusion that, according to Accenture, costs US businesses over $1 trillion annually due to employee disengagement, low productivity, and high turnover. Even worse, most businesses aren't looking for these costs. The enduring value of belonging that we teach organizational and people leaders to build at work cannot be understated: These are the leaders willing to try something new, something that places them outside their comfort zones in the hope of making a real transformation and becoming the leaders they need to be to navigate these times.

Initially, too many of these leaders didn't believe building belonging spaces were even necessary. Some falsely believed they would foster division. We encourage these leaders to recognize the enormous responsibility they have in creating cultures of belonging and how they can begin building them by ensuring a shared sense of team safety and trust at all levels of their organizations. Without it, the power of belonging will remain elusive at work, and certainly in our society.

You may be at any stage in recognizing the importance of feeling a sense of belonging, beyond just *thinking* about it as a never-ending internal dialogue. Intellectual awareness is one level of understanding it. A deeper felt sense of belonging requires fully seeing it, hearing it, smelling it, touching it, and tasting it. That sensory level of belonging is what this book will help you experience through Kelli's expert storytelling abilities. In the process, you'll gain an embodied sense of what it means to belong, while increasing your possibilities of truly feeling it through connecting with Kelli's journey to find hers.

Great leaders like Kelli Houston teach us that learning is a constant process. For me, that realization was reaffirmed in 2017 when I met her, and she is now a cherished colleague and good friend. Our evolving relationship continues to teach me new and important lessons, and it's for this reason that I'm so grateful you'll be able to experience her wisdom too!

Rhodes Perry

Founder and CEO, The Belonging Movement

Introduction: Outed

It was supposed to be just another day. I was finally leaving my parents' house to start a new life in Los Angeles. I was nineteen years old and still reckoning with my sexuality. Over the summer, I had met a girl (an acquaintance of my old high school friends' group) who would change my life in ways that were yet unfathomable. It was my first real connection with another girl who made my brain think, *Could this be one?* We met over the summer break and had instant chemistry, well at least sexually. Just about every day that summer, we spent it together. We couldn't get enough of each other, and every day when we went home, we knew we'd see each other the next day. It was the type of relationship I dreamed of.

It was my final day in Reno, and as I prepared to leave for my flight, everything fell apart. The day started beautifully; we spent time in the morning at the safe house (as I call it), where the two of us could be together without interruption. Knowing this was the last time we were going to be with each other for a while, we wanted to spend as much time together as possible. We exchanged gifts, hers a silver bracelet, mine a heart locket with our names engraved in the gold framing. "I don't want this to end," she said as though she could read my mind. I didn't want it to end either, and my mind wandered to how I could scheme a plan to stay or at least make a promise to write or call, anything to stay connected. In the days before texting or social media, we did it the old-fashioned way: You just called until some weird answering machine picked up.

As the sun started to come down, it was time for us to part ways. She drove me back to my house, where we both thought it would be an innocent drop-off. However, I insisted that she come in to talk for a minute. I wanted to hang on to this moment and this person who was helping me step into my own sexuality.

Assuming my parents would be gone for a while, I said, "We should have the place to ourselves, but you never know." I showed her around for a bit, a quick view, as the house was 1,100 square feet. About a minute later, I told her I had to grab something out of my mom's room and asked her to wait outside. She didn't listen and promptly followed me, which initially annoyed me. But one thing led to another, as things so often do in a young queer relationship, and suddenly we were making out in the bedroom. I was lost in the moment, thinking about having to leave this girl and my family and go to a new city I had only glimpsed years before.

After what felt like forever, I sensed the bedroom door slightly creak open. The moment I heard it, I already knew what happened, and I freaked. My heart dropped to the pit of my stomach as I jumped up with my eyes wide open, looking at who was at the door. It was my dad! No words were spoken, as there was no denying what was happening, and no excuse in the world could make him believe what he'd seen wasn't real.

My blood turned cold, and we quickly jumped up. She was completely oblivious to everything, and I had to explain to her that my dad had just caught us. She hadn't seen anything, but I knew my dad; he always pulled some sneaky prank just to get a reaction from the person he was sneaking up on. I raced down to the living room where all my boxes and luggage were, but they were all gone, along with my dad.

I started to put two and two together and realized that the only place they could've gone was to the airport. Since this girl was now the only one of us who had a car, I told her we needed to get to the airport now! As we raced out of the house and to the airport, I couldn't believe what was happening to me. I didn't know what was going to be waiting for me when we got there, but I knew it wasn't going to be good.

After sitting in her car for what felt like years, lost in my own thoughts and dreading what was waiting for us, we pulled up at Reno's football-field-length of an airport, and suddenly she looked toward the opposite end of the drop-off area. "Hey, isn't that your stuff over there?" she asked while pointing to the boxes I had laid out in my parents' house and was taking with me. Yes, that was my stuff, but my dad wasn't there. All my luggage had been dropped off at the side of the airport terminal. It was a message my dad wanted to send me and his response to finding out I was gay. He couldn't process or understand what he'd just seen, and this was his way of showing his disapproval.

I was astonished. I was confused. I couldn't believe what just happened. It didn't feel real, and I tried so hard to believe it wasn't. This had to be some bad dream I was bound to wake up from soon. I couldn't stop myself from freaking out. I didn't know what I was supposed to do, what I could do at that moment. All I had in front of me was this girl, a plane that was going to take off soon, and my luggage sitting outside the airport. I said my goodbyes, and the entire flight I was freaking out, from checking in to getting on the plane and especially getting off the plane, where my sister was supposed to pick me up. I'd been outed by a girl I used to know. In the crowded airport, I asked out loud, "What other shitstorm lies before me?"

Chapter 1

The Miracle Baby

Spring 1971

From the moment I was born, I was seen as the miracle baby of my family. Not because of any grand miracle I was going to bestow upon my family by being born, but because it was a miracle I survived at all.

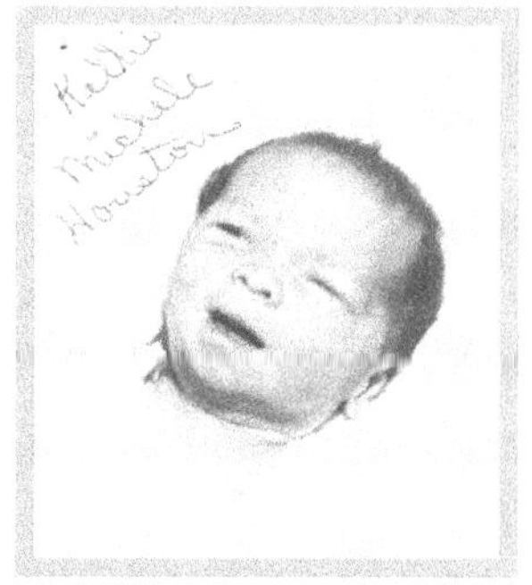

As the story goes and has been told to me, I wasn't expected to be born for another month. As was typical in the Houston household, my mom had been very involved with the constant care of my older brother and sister, who at the time were about ten and eight years old, respectively. One day in mid-April, she slipped on the cold kitchen floor and began to contract while losing a considerable amount of blood. My sister tried to help her but was flustered and, as an eight-year-old, had no idea what to do except call an ambulance. My dad wasn't home at the time, so my mom, sister, and brother were taken to the ER together.

The entire time, my mom was terrified with thoughts that her pregnancy could be in jeopardy and that something had happened to me or there was going to be some complication, given the amount of blood she felt she had lost at home. After the doctors at the hospital treated her wound and ran a check to see if I was impacted, they assured her that all was well, at least in the best way it could be in 1971 medical systems. They wanted to keep her overnight for observation, and at that point my dad had joined my brother and sister in the waiting room, along with my maternal grandmother.

To everyone's shock, I arrived at 10:30 a.m. on Monday, April 19, 1971. The methods leading up to the delivery seemed to go well, but her doctor began to worry immediately following the delivery. I had a soft whimper of a "coo," weighed only four pounds, nine ounces, and was having difficulty breathing on my own. The doctors quickly intubated me, which kept me alive, but they weren't sure what was going to happen, how I would come out of this, if at all. As the doctors and nurses scrambled around, a sense of dread came over the waiting room. They all knew there was nothing they could do except wait and hope that I would be okay.

Then my grandmother took things into her own hands. I'm still not exactly sure how she was able to get into the room where I was, but she made her way in. I was later told that she saw all the tubes as I lay in the oval incubator, and she proceeded to pray over my frail little body. Once she finished her prayer and was on her way out of the room, the doctors began to see movement from me as I cooed and murmured. The nurse noticed I'd finally begun to breathe on my own, so staff proceeded with the whole 1970s medical pat on the back thing, and like a miracle, I was able to breathe. From that day forward, I was deemed the miracle baby.

Unfortunately, that didn't mean it was the end of the health complications I had growing up, but I was on the earth and life was about to begin.

Family Matters, Summer 1974

Being seen as the miracle baby of my family didn't allow me any perks such as a car or private suite. It honestly felt more like a detriment than an actual title I wanted to have. I'm sure because of everything that happened, all the stress and worry about whether I was going to be born okay, my mom became what is today called a helicopter mom. As I grew older, it felt comforting to have someone looking out for me, but as one nears forty that can become a problem. But I digress. As I look back, I realize how important it was to have a parent who really cared for and loved me enough to ensure I didn't get hurt. It's funny how much you miss that support as you age.

It started when I was in kindergarten. She would walk me to and from school every day, making sure no terrifying kidnappers would jump out of the bushes and take me away like a scene from a 1970s after-school special, even though the school was literally up the street. Mom was very protective. After a terrifying pregnancy and me being the baby of the family (literally at the time and figuratively), she wanted to ensure I was safe and sound. Any time she didn't know where I was or what I was doing, she'd send my brother or another family member to come and find me. There are many stories of my harrowing escapes as a child, when I would disappear only to be found safe. One of those stories involved a shopping trip to the local Kmart.

I was a precocious three-year-old and wandered away from the family to go look at the toy section, not telling anyone where I was going. After about two minutes, they realized I was missing. Panic ensued, and my mom sent my brother as the search party to go find me. He wandered through the aisles, calling out my name. Meanwhile my mom and my aunt saw a little glimpse of me running up and down the aisles; the only way they knew it was me was because my pigtails were flying around everywhere. Finally, my brother tracked me down as I gleefully ran to him, and thus the Kmart crisis came to a dramatic close.

When we arrived home, my sister asked Mom why she was so terrified. She simply responded, "Do you know what would've happened to us if we didn't come back to this house without Kelli? Your father would've dropped us off at a Kmart."

My parents were reacting to the darkest times of the 1970s and '80s, also known as the milk carton generation, with missing and exploited children across the country. My mom often remarked of her annoyance when people in the community would walk up to my stroller and say, "What a pretty baby" or "Her hair is so beautiful." What seemed like a simple compliment for her child was actually a secret message with the intent of stealing me away from her. Who could blame her? If I'd ever been a parent, I might've been equally concerned. I imagine in her mind it was as if she had to assemble a search party and find me quickly before the worst happened. Unfortunately for her mental health, I was an explorer and would constantly wander off and, well . . . explore.

My brother, Robert, was the empathetic one and looked after me in those early years. He was the one who'd take me on whatever adventure he had planned. He looked after me and listened to whatever may have been on my mind, patient and always caring. Born in early 1961, he became the star of the family through his academic talents. It also didn't hurt to be the firstborn and a boy. He was named after my father, with the exception of his middle name. He was a dynamic student, quiet yet ambitious, and one of the most thoughtful young men I ever knew prior to the birth of my nephews.

In high school, Robert was heavily involved in any academic project available and became the first Black student body president, the first one in the family to be accepted into two big Ivy League colleges, Princeton and Stanford. Eventually he selected Stanford so he could stay closer to home and spend time with our grandparents, who lived in San Jose. The irony was that at heart he was a sensitive, kind, and loving brother and, above all, was one of my best friends growing up. Our attachment seemed to come from the fact that he was the one who named me after I was born. He was present during my birth and helped my parents come up with my name after thinking of a perfect "K" name. He was also smart enough to have the premonition that there would be a generation of "Kellys," so he had the wherewithal to spell it with an "I," which at the time was unique, and I am proud to keep that spelling today.

My sister, Kim, was born in the year of JFK Jr.'s assassination, in February 1963. She was every bit a Pisces: creative, outgoing, and family oriented. She was compassionate and intuitive, but on the other hand seemed to not really want me around, or at least that was what I thought growing up. As a child, I believed she was happiest when it was just her and my brother, based on the stories told around the dinner table. As much as I love her, those feelings persisted as I grew older and made it difficult for us to build a sisterhood.

According to Mom, when my brother and sister found out she was pregnant with me, Robert couldn't wait to have another little sister, while Kim took the news very hard, even asking, "Why can't we give her back?" Looking back, I don't think she hated me, but she was certainly not happy being the middle child. I think in her own eight-year-old mind, she knew that meant I would be the center of attention, and that had to have been frustrating. She was smart. Nonetheless, it affected our relationship for years after my birth and during my adolescent years.

Even though there were some powerful women in my family, including my grandmother, there was always this fixation on what the men were doing and what they had done. My immediate family was the typical nuclear family environment, where Mom stayed at home to raise the kids while Dad was the breadwinner and made sure there was food on the table.

Dad always made sure he provided for our family, and as a kid I looked up to him. A trailblazer in his own right, Dad was the first Black police officer in Reno, which came with its own costs. Being the first Black police officer in 1962 meant the resistance against him was immense. Among the other cops, there had been a campaign to oust him. The idea was that they would put him in as many dangerous, life-threatening situations or calls as possible to hopefully drive him away. Any time a call came through where the suspect might be armed and dangerous, they would send him with little backup. It affected him so much that after about a year and a half of service, he quit the force for good. I'm sure his decision was coupled with the fact that my mom was terrified for both him and for me, the baby they just had, and he didn't want his children to grow up without a dad. Still, he made history and I'm proud to tell his story. Years later, my handsome and smart nephew, Jarred, inspired by his grandfather's heroism, became a police officer in honor of the man he admired so much.

The glue that held all my family together was my grandmother. Her number one goal was to make sure that the family was a unit. She kept everyone together and impacted our definitions of what it meant to be a family. She was a strong, funny, intelligent woman of faith who generated a tremendous amount of respect from the family because of those qualities. Everyone loved my grandmother, and she loved everybody. She saw herself as everyone's mother even if she didn't give birth to them, and she had true, unconditional love for all of us. I learned self-respect from my grandmother. She taught me and my siblings to never let someone tell us we are less than and that there wasn't anything we couldn't do. She saw each of us as special children.

Dad made it a point for all of us to spend as much time as possible with my grandmother. Most of his family lived in Mississippi, so he didn't have a lot of family to rely on and was extremely close with my maternal grandmother when they were both alive. Grandmother Brooks viewed my father like a son, and Dad wanted each of us to have that special bond with her as well. Countless weekends were spent traveling across the country to California to see and spend time with this incredible woman.

From the time I started elementary school until her debilitating stroke, my grandmother would travel to Reno to take me clothes shopping before every school year. Those memories of being able to go with her and bond with her are some I hold close to my heart. We bonded together during those trips, and she shared wisdom and her sense of humor with me, encouraging me and listening to whatever was on my mind at the time. She was a huge mentor for me growing up, and she left an indelible mark on me even before

I knew it. She was the one who prayed over me when I was born, and she saw something special in me that I didn't see for myself until decades later.

Health Complications, Fall 1975

When I was about three years old, though I don't remember the exact specifics of how it happened, I experienced a traumatic event that changed my life forever. While watching a Little League baseball game with Dad, I was inadvertently hit in the head with a baseball. It was one of those one-in-a-million shots, and unfortunately I was hit. My father rushed me to the hospital. Mom, of course, was beside herself with grief, worrying what else could've happened to me because of this and immediately taking me to the pediatrician to make sure I was okay.

It was only during this examination with my pediatrician that they all realized I wasn't responding to hearing cues. Although I showed a good score with my left ear, my right showed little to no response, which meant I was approximately 80–90 percent deaf in the right ear. This was something that stumped them since there had been no history of hearing loss from the time of my birth until now. Immediately, I was diagnosed as officially deaf in my right ear.

Given the limited medical tech in those days, my pediatrician wasn't sure whether my deafness was caused at birth or by the fierce hit to the head by a baseball, but the overall medical outcome came down to the fact that either could've led to the hearing loss. Many other factors could've contributed to my hearing loss, one being that as a preemie born in the 1970s, intubating me when my breathing stopped could've exacerbated my hearing loss. Either way, this diagnosis changed my entire way of life.

Growing up, I don't think anyone ever said it was a disability, but it felt like I was different. And it wasn't just a thought; I could see I was being treated differently. It became more difficult for me to grasp what people were saying, and it was obvious at the time because I'd position myself to always sit on the left side of a person so I could listen to them closely and more intently. I had to teach myself how to read lips and pick up on people's body language to interact with them better. I had to go through all these extra hoops just because of how I was born, and no one around me knew what that was like, to have to do so much more just to communicate.

Throughout grade school and into high school, I felt my hearing loss was a part of myself I had to hide in order to gain acceptance from everyone in my life. Mom and Robert were the ones I confided in. They helped me through those early years, but even at toddler age, I wanted to feel like I could stand on my own two feet.

Look, No Hands! Spring 1976

Because I wanted to have a sense of independence without the responsibilities that came with being an adult, I wanted to get out and away from my parents' house. Even at a young age, I could tell what I was feeling was physical anxiousness to go somewhere. I didn't care where, as long as it was somewhere, which manifested as a fascination with cars.

My earliest memory of driving is when I was three years old. My aunt told me I always said "Draw! Draw!" since I was three and couldn't pronounce "drive," but I wanted to do it, and my aunt was only too eager to oblige. For some reason, she thought it was the best decision to help keep that passion going in my little heart by putting me in her lap while we were driving. She'd put my hands on the steering wheel and keep her feet on the pedals. At three years old, I couldn't even say "drive," but I was driving, so I guess you could say I was eager to get behind the wheel. It only lasted a few minutes, but it gave me the best three-year-old thrill a person that age could have. I was driving!

My passion for driving only ignited since that moment. After that time, I'd sit behind my dad and mimic his actions, copying everything he was doing even if I didn't know what I was doing or why. It got to the point where he took a steering wheel off an old truck and gave it to me to use when he drove. I sat behind him in the car, and whenever he turned left, I turned my own wheel left. Whenever he pressed the brakes, I pressed my fictional brake pedal, and whenever he changed gears, I changed mine, even though I had no idea what the lever he moved even did.

I continued to do this until I was about ten or eleven years old, as it gave me a sense of agency and independence I wouldn't otherwise have had at such a young age. Even though I was in the back seat, I was the one in control in my head, going to some different place outside of the area I could see from the confines of my home. It was my way of getting the independence I wanted and needed, "free" to go to some new place. Usually it was just for groceries or something mundane, but soon it was church.

The Call of Church, Summer 1976

When I turned six years old, Mom decided it was time for me to start going to church. She was very spiritual and became more so once she was reintroduced to the church after my birth. She found comfort in being in the sanctuary of our neighborhood church. We had known the pastor and his wife since my birth, and their family became a permanent and gratifying fixture for the remainder of our lives. The church community became another family unit, and just like other Black families around the country, we attended services on a consistent basis. At the time, it felt like there were never-ending services and activities, interrupted only by play time. There was vacation Bible school, Sunday school, and evening church, so we were in church at least twice a week. Mom had every intention of ensuring that her children were saved, and Robert especially became heavily involved, as he aspired to become a minister himself one day. Given the influence from my grandmother, that dream eventually came true.

Grandmother Brooks was the "mother" of the church in San Jose, and we visited her regularly. She lived only about two hours away from us, so almost every weekend and every summer break we went to visit her or she came to visit us. Every visit, we inevitably went to church. It felt like there was never a reprieve.

While Robert felt a call to the church, I was the complete opposite. The only ministry I was interested in was perfecting the ministry of sleeping in. While I loved God and my church, I felt as any six-year-old would, uninterested in going to a place of worship. Oftentimes, I came up with all sorts of excuses to try to get out of going, such as trying to fake, as best I could, being sick. Every time, I was like, *Do I make this seem like I'm about to die so that I don't have to go to church?* One way was to drink a ton of fluids the night before and try to hog the one bathroom in the house and pretend I had a stomachache. But by the time I'd get to the bathroom, my mom would be occupying the entirety of it to get ready for church, and by that time my stomach actually did hurt.

I'm not sure why I resisted church, other than I hated doing something that felt forced. I also recognized something in me that made it difficult to focus on the institution of religion. At an early age, I acknowledged how different I felt from the other church kids, and I didn't understand why I couldn't get along with them. I had no one to tell of my curiosity. I couldn't just outright tell my parents how I was feeling, especially Mom, as she brushed it off with a quick, "It's what we do; we go to church." I needed to stay on God's path, and there would be no talking my way out of going. The guilt was greater than the stomach pain.

As I continued to get older and learn more about the church, it pushed me further away from it. I could see the hypocrisy of the church. It was frustrating for me to see as I was growing up that it was okay for people to say one thing and do another. They preach "Love thy neighbor" but then say that applies only to certain people. This was especially true as I began to question my sexuality.

When I was in second grade, I began experiencing my first lesbian crush, which was on my teacher Mrs. Anderson. At the time, I didn't know how to put it into words or even what it was exactly, but I felt this different feeling whenever she paid attention to me. In my head it was her giving me special attention, perceived special attention really, that made me gravitate toward her and feel something I hadn't felt before. At the time, no one talked about these types of things. In the 1970s and '80s, talk of being gay or queer, let alone relationships among them, were taboo. I was left by myself to question what I was feeling and why I was feeling it.

As I became a young adolescent, there were expectations that I'd soon start to develop interest in the boys in my class or in my neighborhood, but that never happened. I heard rhetoric from the church saying that gay and queer people are terrible and the epitome of the devil, yet God supposedly loves everyone. These conflicting messages made me doubt that what I was feeling was real. Maybe it would just pass and I wouldn't feel this way anymore. "Pray away the gay" as they say.

But it didn't go away. What persisted were my conflicted feelings about being in an institution that was teaching me and everyone else that my thoughts, feelings, and my very being were wrong in some way. So I continued to resist where I could, hoping I wouldn't have to go back to church. Hoping that each time I faked an illness or made some excuse, I could just go back to sleep. Hoping that when I woke up, I wouldn't have to fake it anymore.

Chapter 2

What Is Love?

Alone in the Neighborhood, Spring 1983

While I was growing up, my dad continued to be a pillar of the community. He sought to make a better life for his kids by providing for them as well as for the neighborhood kids. He was seen as a very tough yet thoughtful contributor to advancing the rights of his Black and other non-White neighbors, like a disciplinarian but more of a hero. People really looked up to and respected him.

In early 1971, my dad worked with several community leaders to create an NAACP chapter in Northern Nevada, and in late 1975, when he saw that kids of color were being forced to swim outside their own neighborhoods, he helped develop a community pool across the street from our house. He also helped create Reno's basketball league for all, regardless of their race, making sure the kids in the neighborhood had the same opportunities as their counterparts in wealthier communities. He was firm with other kids in the neighborhood, but he showed how much he cared by being there and trying to support those around him. All this garnered him a reputation among the other families; in the neighborhood, the name Houston was synonymous with community leader, and you didn't mess with Mr. Houston's kids. My dad wanted to help everyone, to help save them, and seeing him do that for everyone is partially what set me on the path to where I am now.

I don't know what the experiences were for my brother or sister growing up through elementary school, but the irony is that, for me, the name Houston didn't protect me. I felt the jealousy of my peers, especially kids in the neighborhood who resorted to a light form of bullying. Whether it was in school or church, I was teased and taunted for the way I spoke due to being deaf in one ear. It took years for me to develop the skills needed to talk and respond "normally" when I had a conversation with someone.

Not only was it hard for me to hear and respond to people, but my eyesight wasn't that great either, so I had to wear glasses when I was growing up. With these issues combined, I needed to be at the front of the class, and I was constantly called a teacher's pet because teachers needed to check in with me to make sure I had what I needed. To everyone else in class, this special attention was just more fuel for the fire. I felt I needed to bottle my feelings of anger and frustration, as well as my plain fear of speaking up for the injustices I felt had befallen me at such a young age. I retreated, and it took years of therapy to finally reconcile the feelings of loneliness that I experienced in my preteen years.

All of this was compounded by the fact that the kids in the neighborhood appeared to be jealous of how complete my family looked. I was never a latchkey kid. I always had at least one parent in the house when I came home, and with my dad being the community figure he was, I think the other kids wished they had what I had. A lot of them grew up with only one parent, or someone in their family struggled with addiction. Compared with them, we were seen as the perfect nuclear family. Both of my parents made sure that all their kids were provided for, and we were encouraged to go to school and eventually college. On the outside it seemed like we had everything. Materially we did have a lot growing up, but there were issues within my family that I didn't know about or didn't realize until I got older.

Coupled with all the special treatment I was given, the other kids likely thought that I thought I was better than them. The way I spoke and acted was, to them, as if I were a White kid, like someone who thought they were above the rest of the kids in the school and the neighborhood, and they desperately wanted to keep me down. But I never saw myself as above anyone. I was a kid who was struggling, trying to figure out why it was so difficult to make friends and how to deal with other internal turmoil that would affect me for years to come.

I felt more and more isolated, and I hated going to school or anywhere that somehow involved the neighborhood kids. It was like a constant hailstorm outside, and there wasn't any way to avoid it. In school, in church, and in the neighborhood, I couldn't get away from the harassment and bullying. Even the kids I considered friends at the time would chime in when some of the other kids made fun of me. Whenever I did try to engage with or be around them, they pushed me away or came up with their own excuses, such as that I didn't come from the "their" neighborhood, even though I was raised in virtually the same place. We were all raised in the same kind of lower-middle class neighborhoods, so I knew their excuses were bullshit, but there wasn't much I could do. I tried to fit in but was always pushed away, and even at an early age I felt the hypocrisy of some of the other Black kids around me and how they treated those who were different. They treated me almost as if they were social distancing; whenever I was around, everyone else was at least six feet away.

Because of all this, I didn't feel connected to the community around me. I am a woman of color, and association is part of my connection to the Black community. Due in part to my childhood experiences, I felt like the "white sheep." I never formed any real connections with the other kids, even those who shared a similar skin tone to my own.

Once I got through elementary school, I was left with a choice: I could go to either the middle school across from my street or to a different middle school. I didn't think twice about it. I wanted to get out of the area, and so I decided to go to the school that was on the other side of Reno. I talked with my parents about the decision, and they agreed this would be the best way forward for me.

It was a new school and a new start for me. I was nervous about what would happen, but I was quickly distracted.

Summer Fun, 1983

The summer before middle school, there was a program for the kids of Reno called "Summer Fun." It was like a summer camp with a bunch of different activities that were planned out each day, from intramural sports to going out on the lake. Each day was packed with activities for us to do, and much of the program was run by my dad since he was working for Reno Parks and Rec. He encouraged me to join, and it was an incredible experience, one I kept going back to until I was a sophomore in high school.

Kids from all over Reno attended the program, and I got to meet all sorts of different people I hadn't seen before. My first time there, I met another Kelly, who changed my outlook on life at the time. Kelly was a White boy who lived on the other side of town. It was a great experience for me to meet someone who lived outside of my neighborhood and someone who didn't look like everyone else I knew. He was a bit taller than me and had blond hair and blue eyes, just a really cute guy. We became fast friends through the program, and we had a great time getting to know each other and spend time together.

One day, Kelly rode his bike across Reno to come hang out with me. We took our bikes and headed toward the middle school I was supposed to go to, the one right across the street. Just behind the school was a huge playground with a tennis court, basketball court, and town-themed playset. We made our way toward the built-in bleachers of the tennis court and talked as twelve-year-olds would. As we were talking about school and the program, he suddenly stepped in front of me. I was surprised but I stopped. I don't remember what he said or how he said it, but he leaned in for a kiss. I was shocked and couldn't believe this was happening, but I also felt very open and vulnerable. It was a feeling I hadn't felt before, and it felt good that he liked someone like me. I never felt attractive, and my self-esteem was buried beneath years of constantly being made fun of or avoided. To have a cute boy like him wanting to kiss me made me feel over the moon. We made out for a pretty long time and, for one of the first times, I felt okay in my body.

The moment was cut short when I started to freak out that my parents didn't know where I was. As usual, the family search party was on high alert with my parents as I explained to Kelly and quickly made my way back home. The school was visible from my parents' house, and Dad was sitting outside. He was about to come look for me when I rounded the corner of the school and he saw me. There was no getting around it. We both saw each other, and like a dog with her tail tucked between her legs, I slowly made my way toward him. He gave me a disapproving look, and I tried my best not to make eye contact with him. I was scared, knowing I was in trouble.

He glared at me with both relief that his child was safe and the stern look that comes from worrying. "You know we've been looking for you," he said.

I kept my eyes focused on the ground and said, "I'm sorry, Dad. I was just riding my bike with a friend."

He dug into me deeper. "Well, where were you riding?"

I kept searching for something to look at other than my dad's looming figure. "I was riding around the school across the street."

I tried to pass it off as best as I could, hoping I wouldn't get punished terribly for not showing up on time or letting them know where I was. Thankfully, my dad was merciful. I don't think he had the heart to carry out any serious punishment, but he made sure I knew not to do it again. Of course being a kid, I did do it again, except I was a lot more mindful of the time so that I wouldn't be caught as easily.

When I had a moment by myself, I couldn't stop thinking about Kelly and that moment with him. As an imaginative twelve-year-old, I had the immediate thought, *I'm going to marry him. He's the one.* I'd draw our initials together in heart shapes, write our names on all sorts of papers, and daydream about the future together with him and what we'd do next.

Being attracted to Kelly was what I called "acceptable feelings." It was what I was taught was right and what I "should" be feeling. For a time, I started to think it was okay to be with a boy. This one was helping me bring out feelings of intimacy and normalcy for the first time, and it felt good, as if things were finally heading in the right direction. After being told that being with a girl was wrong, this was like a course correction. The feelings I'd felt before must have been fake or something else, because now I was falling for Kelly. This was normal. *This is how I'm supposed to feel, right?* Well, the intimacy I had with him felt right for all I knew back then, and I equated that to love.

As the summer went on, we'd meet up daily. In public we acted like a bunch of kids, running around and having fun with each other, but in private we talked, kissed, and were a lot more intimate with each other. It was one of the first times and one of the first people I felt comfortable with. I could be intimate with Kelly and also be myself. He didn't judge me or look down on me in any way, and it felt great to spend time with him.

Our relationship lasted until the summer's end. When school started back up in September, we went to our respective middle schools and lost touch with one another. There wasn't a big breakup moment or anything like that, we just ended up going to two different schools and drifted apart. Without seeing each other every week and focusing on school, things ended naturally, and we both moved on.

My attention slowly went from daydreaming about getting married to this cute boy to trying to fit in and get involved with this new environment I was entering. If there's one thing that Summer Fun and that summer specifically helped me with, it was stepping into my own self and building my self-confidence. I made some friends in the program and had my first kiss. I finally felt like I fit in. I wanted to keep that positive momentum going, and I made it a point to put myself out there.

New Environment, Lasting Friendships, Fall 1984

Going to middle school, I was glad to be free of Mom's grasp. Her constant monitoring continued as I got older, and the older I got, the more rules and restrictions she added. I always had to tell her where I was and where I was going, and until I was on my own I couldn't stay over at a friend's house nor go out on any national holiday.

Two things were going through my mind as I was on my first bus ride to the middle school across the city. First, I was glad I was finally free from the surveillance state of my mom. From the time I got on the bus to school to the time I came back to my house on that same bus, I finally had a little bit of independence. It wasn't much, but I was glad to get even the tiniest bit of leniency during the school week.

Second, coming from Summer Fun, I felt more confident in myself and was finally able to explore different parts of me, such as what I liked, what I enjoyed doing, and how to make real connections with other people. That didn't mean everyone there would welcome me with open arms, and I thought about what it would be like once I got there. What would this new school look like for me? It was located in the "nicer" part of Reno, and I hoped the kids there would treat me with at least a fraction more respect than the kids in my neighborhood did.

The first thing I noticed and knew about this middle school was that it was predominately White. When I say that, I don't mean that it was about 70 percent White; I mean that me and about two or three other kids were the only people of color. Everyone there was either White or White-presenting. The irony was that I actually fit in more with this group of kids than with the ones in my own neighborhood. They didn't treat me any differently than anyone else, and I never got the sense I was being treated as an outsider. I fit in.

Looking back at everything, I know it was code switching (switching between different ways of speaking depending on the group of people you're around) that helped me fit in with the people around me. At the time, however, I didn't know this. How I spoke was formed from my family, and hearing other people speak with the same dialectic and tones I was raised hearing gave me an ironic sense of belonging. Fitting in with these kids gave me reassurance that I was able to explore not only the school but also myself.

As soon as I got into my first classes, I wanted to get acclimated and keep trying different things. I took a lot of different electives such as art and band, even though I wasn't very good at either of them. I even tried out for sports, including tennis and basketball. Like a kid in a candy store, I wanted to try everything, taking little bits of different pieces. Even if I didn't like them, at least I tried.

When it came to lunchtime, I quickly found out there were a lot of kids who'd get up from their seats at a certain time. I asked someone where everyone was going, and they told me that a bunch of kids go outside around the corner to dance. By this time, the movie *Breakin'* had come out, a breakdancing film that, especially for kids, towers over classics such as *Grapes of Wrath*. I love this movie, and when it came out, we all tried to copy the moves we saw, including spinning on our backs and heads, which led to many of us having arthritis today.

One day, I followed the kids outside to watch what they were doing. They had all formed a massive circle in a field near the cafeteria. One of the teachers was supervising everyone and had even brought a music speaker for all the kids to dance to. One at a time, each kid in the circle made their way to the center to show off some of their moves. Everyone was singing or moving their bodies in place as we all cheered on the person in the middle until they finished their routine before molding back into the dance circle. The kids were really good dancers; I learned how to dance from them, and soon I was popping and locking with the best of them, at least by Reno standards. It felt like a perfect opportunity to connect with other kids, so I made my way into the circle. The other kids gladly expanded the ring to allow me to join in on the fun, and as I slowly worked up the courage to show off my best moves, the only moves I'd picked up and knew at the time, the "Lock and Drop," I realized I was fairly good at picking up dance moves with ease.

There were no expectations on any of us to put on a show or seriously perform; it was just a bunch of kids letting loose and having fun. After that first lunch period, I went outside every lunch break and danced. It's one of the most vivid memories I have of this time because it felt so carefree and fun. Not having any expectations and just being you, whatever that may be, was cheered on by the rest of the kids in the circle. Even now, those moments bring me a sense of peace for what it was like to be that age and just be your own person, even if I didn't even know what that meant at the time. Those moments also helped boost my confidence and got me to keep putting myself out there.

I was soon taking several different classes I normally wouldn't have even considered. Though I was never good at either of them, I took art class and band, and they turned out to be where I met some of my closest friends. In art class, I quickly discovered I was not very good at sketching, nor anything that had to do with making art, but luckily I had an amazing art teacher who always encouraged his students regardless of what they created. He gave me the nickname "Special K," which was endearing to me and made me feel special.

In all my classes, I considered myself the jokester, always trying to make people laugh. Whether it was making some side comment to what someone said or commenting on the day's events with comedic timing, I had a knack for getting people to laugh. I realized that if there's one person people like to be around, it's someone who can get them to laugh. That was how I was able to start to form connections with people.

One day in art class, I was sitting next to two girls and cracked some joke that got them both to laugh. They turned to me and introduced themselves as Angie and Jasmine, and we became fast friends from that point on. Angie was a heavyset girl who was painfully shy, kept her head down, and never really talked to anyone, but she was the sweetest girl I'd ever met up to that point in my life. Jasmine was a pretty, tall, blonde who was very similar to Angie in that she was also sweet but seemed insecure with herself. Both of them had a desire to fit in and be with the popular kids in our school.

The irony was that only a year prior, I was in their position, shy and quiet, but now I was putting myself out there in this new environment and slowly becoming one of the more popular kids in school. I got along with just about everyone, and everyone seemed to enjoy it when I was around and cracking jokes. I wanted the same for Angie and Jasmine and pushed us to go out constantly, whether it was going to the mall or to after-school events. I wanted to experience everything I could in the time that I had, and I loved doing it with both of them.

All three of us clicked right away. They were two of my closest friends in middle school. We all preferred the same music, which at the time was considered New Wave, including bands such as The Cure and Depeche Mode. Keep in mind this was the era of MTV, back when it actually did what its acronym promised: broadcasting music videos on the small screen twenty-four hours a day. One of the biggest bands we got into was Duran Duran. We were all Duran

Duran fiends and obsessed over who our favorite member was. Jasmine liked Nick, Angie obsessed over Simon, and I liked John Taylor. They became our main topic of discussion, with talk of nothing but Simon, John, and Nick day after day. Whenever a new music video premiered, we all went crazy, enraptured by the elegance of yachting in "Rio" or the punk style approach of "Planet Earth," both of which we watched on repeat. We swapped stories about their love lives and what life would be like if we were "Mrs. Duran Duran." Seventh grade innocence at its best.

Soon after we met, we started making appearances at the local mall (a trend that would last until the early '90s), introducing each other to our parents, and going to each other's houses. My parents were thrilled that I was making new friends, and they could see I was starting to thrive in this new environment. It was an extremely gratifying feeling, and having these two friends meant the world to me. After art class ended and we were free to choose different classes, we made sure we took the same classes so that we were always together at some point during school.

More often than not, when all of us hung out together, Jasmine and Angela would get on the topic of bands and talk about "the boys," as we called them. Thinking back now, my obsession was the music more than the boys, but nonetheless, I engaged with a dreamy interpretation of what it meant to be a straight girl who was in love with a boy I could never have. I believe we were in the same category of all teenagers before us who were so connected to a band and its band members that they would fall apart at even just the mention of their name. I now realize how silly it all was, but back then it allowed me to secure friendships that meant more to me than any band member (although I still love Duran Duran and try to catch their shows now that they are kind, older gentlemen).

It was a few days after I had met Jasmine and Angie when I met Manny in the same art class. We were told to pair up together with someone in the class for a project, and I happened to be sitting next to him that day, so we paired up. We started talking, and it seemed like we had good chemistry. I found out that we were from the same neighborhood and that the middle school we were going to, Clayton, was actually really popular. They were accepting kids from all over Reno, and I was having a blast so far.

Once I knew we were from the same neighborhood, Manny and I started to get closer. At first it was just as friends who happened to be in the same neighborhood. We'd take the school bus together and hang out in school and at after-school events, and soon I introduced him to my parents and he introduced me to his. My parents loved having Manny over, and his parents loved having me over.

Much like with most of my life, I soon found myself in a relationship with him. I don't remember quite how it came about, but soon we started calling each other boyfriend and girlfriend. We held hands when we were together, but we never did anything more serious than that. My relationship with Kelly had left me in a confused state where I didn't know what was right for me; I had feelings that being in a relationship with a boy was "correct," the "right thing," what I "should have" done. I know now that those feelings came from being intimate for the first time. Being vulnerable and open to someone in that way was something I'd never experienced before, and while I craved it, I didn't know whether being with a boy was the right thing for me.

To me, Manny was a pillar of strength, someone who didn't judge me for who I was. I felt safe with him, that I could trust him with my whole being even if I didn't know what that meant at the time. He gave me the feeling of security, as I could rely on him when needed and we helped each other along. It was a very reciprocal relationship in which we both enjoyed each other's company and wanted to spend time with one another but just didn't do the things that are traditionally expected in a relationship. We always made sure to take the same classes so we could spend more time together, especially at events that would showcase us as a "couple."

As we prepared for our first prom together, I was in full Aries mode, which meant that I was filled with anticipation of what we would wear and how we would get there given that we were both only thirteen. I planned the entire event, complete with a limo and a frilly pink dress, and Manny would wear a tuxedo. While it might not be the rage in this day and age, our middle-school prom was the event of the year.

When the time came to hire a limo service, I consulted with Jasmine and Angie with a weeklong brainstorm on nothing but limo services in the greater Reno area. At first it was a fun idea as we put in the hours researching how much a rental limo was and where we could possibly rent one. When I brought the idea to my parents, they both said that they couldn't afford to rent a limo. But I brought out all the research and told them that everyone else was getting one, because of course, every other twelve- to fourteen-year-old was getting a limo for prom. Eventually, we worked it out with a split payment between the parents of the kids who were going, and we all rolled up in style in our respective prom dresses and tuxedos.

It was an incredibly fun and liberating experience to be with Manny and my friends. Laughter, music, dance, and punch. What a life! It was a moment and an experience I'd never had the chance to feel before. I could see the change that was happening within me, and I knew I was finally able to grow as a person here. Surrounded by friends and camaraderie, it's a memory that I hold deep in my heart. Even the ridiculous idea of a limo, which we loved so much that we had to get another one for the following year's prom.

❧ ❧ ❧

After a few months, my art class ended, and it was time to move on to a new rotation of elective classes. I opted for band, putting myself further out of my comfort zone. Much like with art class, I was never really good at playing any of the instruments. I tried the saxophone and the viola but was never fantastic at either. Despite that, I decided to keep pushing my boundaries, and I joined the school band's percussion section. I learned to love the drums, particularly the use of a full drum kit, which delighted my parents in the worst way. As I honed my craft as a drummer, I realized that I had found my niche. My music teacher even marveled at how quickly I learned to play even though I could only play by ear and never learned how to read music. Soon I upgraded from playing on my parents' couch to playing on a full drum kit. It was a love that I would carry into my adulthood.

The switch to band also led to my forming another lasting friendship with a fellow band member named Lisa. One day in class, I cracked a joke that caught her attention, and we introduced ourselves. While I played percussion, Lisa was an excellent flutist. We soon found our chemistry with one another, and she quickly became one of my most precious and trusted friends. We traveled together for band, and the more we talked with each other, the more we bonded. She introduced me to tennis, and we played together all the way until college. I was there when she got her driver's license later in high school, and I learned how to make different foods, such as lasagna, with her and her family. The most telling sign of our growing relationship was the fact that my mom loosened her reins with Lisa because she trusted her that much. Lisa was the only person whose house I could spend the night at, and I was surprised that my mom allowed it. But it was a testament to how much she saw Lisa and I being around each other.

I also quickly learned we had similar upbringings. She was the youngest child, and though her closest sibling was her sister, who was only a few years older, she didn't have a close relationship with her or any of her siblings. So when she was by herself, she was quiet and reserved, but when we got together, we brought out the best in each other. Being able to talk to someone about this, someone who got it and understood what it's like to be the youngest kid, was significant for me. Everyone always looks toward the oldest and what they are doing but rarely takes the same amount of energy to see what the middle child is doing, let alone the youngest.

Before I met Lisa, I had no one to talk to about these things; I never even knew I needed and wanted to. My siblings were already off in college, and all eyes were on my brother and what he was going to do once he graduated from Stanford. My sister went to Pepperdine University, and not as much emphasis was given to her, at least from what I could tell. Without a solid connection to either of them now that they were out of the house, I was left trying to figure out where I was supposed to go. What was my path going to look like? Thankfully I now had someone close to me who got it. She understood what it was like, and we opened up to each other, relating our different experiences. Talking with her was very cathartic and helped me move through those thoughts and feelings, and it helped solidify the lasting friendship I made with her.

The Pressure to Succeed, Winter 1985

Throughout my two years of middle school, weirdly enough, the friendships I made never tended to overlap with one another. It was almost as if I were living three separate lives: one with Manny, one with Lisa, and one with Angela and Jasmine. It was never intentional; it was one of those things that just happened to turn out the way it did.

Regardless, each of them helped me in their own ways. Manny helped give me a sense of security and comfort in a relationship. Lisa got me to push my boundaries, introduced me to so many new things in life, and helped me work through some of the emotions I had bottled up since elementary school. Jasmine and Angela were great friends who helped me further come into my own. The more time I spent with the four of them, the more I started feeling better about myself and my environment, and that paid off big time in my studies. For the first time, I was doing well in this new environment. I had become a B+ student and was proud of how well I was doing. I couldn't believe how much I enjoyed going to school every day. It was like I had come out of a dream. Everything seemed to be heading in a positive direction.

As the second year of middle school was approaching its end, I had to start thinking about the future, and not only where I was going to go to high school but what was going to come after. Both my siblings had made the decision to go to college, and my parents heavily encouraged the same from me. Growing up we didn't have a lot. They provided what they could, but it's not like we were living large all the time. My parents provided what they could, and they made sure their kids would have a better life than they had growing up, whether that meant going to college or going into a profession like a trade, something that would help set us up so that we didn't struggle as much later in life.

My brother was destined to go to college, as he was and still is one of the smartest people I know. He excelled in academics the way Michael Jordan excelled on the basketball court. My parents emphasized the importance of an education. My dad had been accepted into Jackson State University in Mississippi on a basketball scholarship, and after a brief stint he decided to join the military. That's where he met my mom, who had a high school education but was just as capable of going on to college as any Black woman in the 1950s. My parents understood that a college education was the best way for people of color to make their own way and not adhere to the racial overtones that affected them pre-civil rights movement. Each Houston child knew that college was the next step and that my parents would do anything to help make it happen for us.

Did I want to go to college? Yes. But the fear of not getting into the best school or not living up to expectations was what drove me to question whether I would excel in college as my siblings did. I was a quiet and introspective student who enjoyed the camaraderie of my schoolmates more than solving an algebra problem.

With the goal of getting into a collegiate college almost set for me, or at least planted within me, I was glad that I was doing better in school, but I didn't have anyone who really guided me. All the times I talked with my brother whenever he came home from college, we never sat down with each other and had a "college talk" where he described what it's like, what to expect, and what to look out for. As I geared up for what high school was going to look like, the question of what would come after loomed in the back of my mind, slowly creeping up until I knew I had to make a decision.

A discussion with my guidance counselor helped me see a path forward. I had been assigned one of the best counselors in school, Mrs. Bond, and I couldn't wait for her to predict my future like a genie in a bottle. "What makes you tick, Kelli?" she asked as she peered over her reading glasses toward me.

"I've always wanted to be a lawyer like Perry Mason," I replied.

She laughed as if to state the obvious, that Perry Mason is a TV character, a man, and White. She of course said none of that, but my Aries brain was working overtime.

Immediately following that meeting, she sent over an aptitude test that was circulating around the high school. It asked questions that helped assess a student's interests, skills, and preferences to help them find a career that would be a good fit. It would be one of many tests I'd take for assistance in my professional journey.

The results of the test returned with three professional options: attorney, teacher, and camp counselor. I elected to go for the camp counselor . . . or did I?

Chapter 3

This Is Me?

Missing Pieces, Spring 1986

While making the transition into high school, the questions that weighed on my mind started to take a toll. I wasn't any closer to answering the questions about my future and my identity, but I kept my struggles inside myself as best I could. I was afraid to talk to others about what I was going through. I didn't know who was safe, which left me thinking in circles about myself. I wasn't making any progress, and I felt no closer to figuring out what I wanted.

The year before high school, the cracks in my compartmentalization started to show. I had a feeling of melancholy that persisted wherever I went. My parents could tell there was something bothering me, but they didn't know how to ask, and I didn't know how to begin to describe it. Even though they didn't know how to help, they did ask whether I wanted to see a therapist, which I agreed to. They didn't have much, and I was able to go to only three sessions, but they helped tremendously. I was scared about feeling lost. What was going to happen in my future? I felt there was something or some part of me that was different, but I didn't know how or why, just that there was something that separated me from the rest of my classmates and my family. Therapy helped me put into words what I was feeling.

I don't remember all the specifics about what we discussed during my first therapy session, but I know it was about family dynamics. I felt extremely out of place within my family, as if I were adopted; there was something about me that made me feel different from the rest of them. Therapy has always been one of the few places I feel comfortable enough expressing these things and just moving my feelings and emotions out of me. Back then it helped me process some of what I was going through internally and allowed me to soundboard off someone who was willing to listen to my internal turmoil.

I expressed to the therapist that I felt different from other people, but I couldn't articulate what that meant without going into specifics. In one session I blurted out, "I think I like girls!" I remember a small gasp coming from across me, and I realized I had made my own therapist stop in her tracks. I wondered what she thought but didn't dare look at her; our eyes never met. I thought, *Now my therapist needs therapy!* While I had always kept the part about me possibly being attracted to other girls a deep secret, I had an explicable urge to say it to someone else so I could make it a true and honest feeling. I never thought about the consequences from that moment, as my young brain was smart enough to know that this privileged information couldn't be shared with my parents. Much to my relief, it never was.

The downside was that based on my parents' insurance coverage, I was covered for only three sessions. Even in the '80s, therapy wasn't cheap, especially since this type of coverage was new for healthcare plans. In the early '70s, my aunt Betty had a breakdown and my family struggled with supporting her in the state of California, where then Governor Ronald Reagan closed the doors to all mental health systems and hospitals, which led to her sinking deeper and deeper into schizophrenia. The memory I have of my grandparents' desperate attempts to find shelter in the form of therapy for my aunt when she was in depths of her crisis was disheartening for everyone in my family to observe. Finally, they agreed to do their best to take care of her by providing her with a home to reside away from the *One Flew Over the Cuckoos' Nest* imprisonment of California's mental institutions at that time.

In the end, my parents didn't have the money to keep paying for my therapy. Even though it was only three sessions, they helped me feel seen. I believe to this day that if I'd stayed in therapy and had ongoing sessions throughout high school, I would've understood the reasons I felt so different from my family a lot sooner than I did. Still, I was grateful my parents cared enough to pay for the therapy and to ask me if I wanted to go talk with someone.

It would take me years to fully understand the importance of those sessions and how they changed my life. It was also one of the few times in my adolescent stage that I appreciated how much my parents cared, and it helped me as I made the transition into high school.

Just a Small-Town Girl, Fall 1986

Going from middle school to high school was both an exciting and anxious transition. I had no idea what to expect, especially in a part of Reno I'd never spent very much time in. It was considered the "rich" part of town, and there was very little reason to find our middle-class family in the area. All I knew were the stories my brother shared with me during his time in high school and how it shaped his and my sister's futures. High school was where they decided on their futures and where I hoped I would decide mine as well. My goal was to ensure I had a future carved out for myself. Since my brother was the student council president and my sister was a cheerleader, they were really popular, and they excelled academically. Due in part to their successes in school, they were both admitted to prestigious colleges, and now, as my time approached, I could feel the pressure. What would I make of my high school experience? Was I going to be as prestigious as the two of them? Their shadows weighed in the back of my mind. I hated the feeling, and it proved to be unhealthy.

Getting into the right high school became a reality thanks to a huge push from my mom. Initially I wanted to go to McQueen High School (a few miles from my middle school) because it was where Lisa had plans to attend, and I wanted to make sure I had a support group since it scared me to think I'd be alone. Mom had other plans for me. She had already identified a school that had recently been awarded the distinction of being one of the best high schools in the Reno metro area according to the *US News & World Report*'s "Best of" series. It was aptly named Reno High School (RHS).

God bless Mom. She always wanted her kids to have more opportunities than she did growing up, so she applied for a school variance transfer so I could attend RHS. For those who may not be familiar, a long, long time ago, if any kid wanted to go to a school that wasn't in their district, their parents had to apply for a variance transfer to attend the school, and the school had to approve them based on various reasons. I applied and was accepted on the basis that "financial, educational, safety, or health conditions would likely be improved by attending a different school." Once my mom got the acceptance letter, my becoming a member of RHS Class of '89 was set in motion.

While not my first choice, it proved to be another pivotal time in my life that yielded joy, hardship, and lasting friendships. Oh, and yes, a first-class education.

I was nervous about starting at a new school and not knowing a soul. Manny and Lisa were going to different schools, and I hadn't connected with Angie and Jasmine since the summer started.

On a brisk morning in September, I was heading to the bus that would take me to my new school, where penny loafers and GTI Volkswagen Cabriolets were plentiful. It was a school of yuppie proportions, but one where, as a budding mini yuppie, I didn't feel completely out of style. When I got to the bus station, Angie and Jasmine were there waiting as well, much to my delight! I couldn't believe they were there. It was a huge feeling of relief for us all to know that we were going to this new school together. We were some of the few who were coming in from outside the area after having been accepted on the school variance program, and it helped to know two of my closest friends were making the journey with me.

Upon our arrival at school, we were greeted by throngs of young adults with feathered hairstyles and dressed in their finest '80s flare. As I observed my surroundings, I had no question that this was a "money school," but I was pleased to know there was a heavy emphasis on academics and making sure the kids who graduated went on to college. RHS also offered students the opportunities to study abroad and to take college classes for early admission, and those with the best grades could earn advanced scholarships.

The difference between the three of us and the other kids became more apparent the more we got to know them. My family was at least comfortable, just not nearly as comfortable as the families of the other kids. Those kids went on ski trips and traveled the country for family vacations, and everyone seemed to own their own cars.

Summer Fun camp and trips to California to visit my grandparents were about as fancy as it got for me in those years.

I stuck close to Angie and Jasmine for a large part of our freshman year. We didn't share any classes, since we had to preregister before the school year started, but we made time for each other when we had it. The three of us relied on each other as we tried to navigate this new world and cemented our friendship. We were the only support system we had when we got there, and we all felt the same way: an outsider within. All the other kids could relate to each other in their own ways, but we could relate only to each other. I felt deep down that we were caught in a vortex of wanting to be something we weren't. We all wanted to feel accepted and welcome among the other kids, it was what we strived for, but we each went after it in different ways. They tried to fit in by appealing to what everyone else valued, whether it was their class status or what they considered popular at the time, while I started to make connections.

In the '80s, most kids in school, including myself, lived a very color-blind existence. We didn't talk about race the way we do today, but it was something I definitely noticed being in an almost all-White high school. There were only a handful of people of color who went to this school at the time, and we sought each other out. It was the first time since middle school that I had friends who were also people of color. It helped a lot to have that diversity and to talk about our experiences. That isn't to say we stuck with each other constantly, but we'd get together every now and then and talk about our aspirations, our hopes, and our experiences. We all wanted to go to college and do something "great" beyond high school, and it was encouraging to see and hear that from people who shared a similar skin tone to mine.

It was great when the handful of people of color were together, but those moments were few and far between, and I wanted to feel accepted by the other kids. I did that by being funny. In a way it allowed my introverted nature to disappear for a short time. I understood that people were moved by laughter and jokes, and I created relationships by finding ways to make others laugh with me. Humor was a safe haven for me in the form of acceptance of my peers. I worked to create relationships with other people who were different from me because it was hard to form connections with other people of color. I felt the safest with the friends around me who had vastly different experiences than I had.

The expectations placed on us growing up were even more intense for our futures. Who and what were we going to be, and what were we going to do when we graduated? Making light of it through self-deprecating humor bridged the Grand Canyon-sized gap between us. All of us were trying to escape from the same place, and humor was really the escape I needed to survive not just high school but also middle school. It brought people together as we joked about our existential dread. Each of us was trying to figure out who we were, trying to form our own identities, even if we didn't understand it at the time. Nobody knew what we were going to do or who we were going to become, but at least we could laugh about it together. That we had in common.

Coming into My Own, Summer 1987

Following my freshman year and into my sophomore year, Mom wanted to get me out of the house more in the summers and to think more broadly about my collegial prospects. She had a friend who was part of Upward Bound, a program with the goal of helping high school students who show potential and aspire to go to college but have difficulty affording the rising costs of education. The program offers students the full college experience (i.e., dorm life, attending classes on campus), as well as my favorite part: meeting college girls. I would not only receive college credit but also a pseudo college experience while I was in high school.

It was my mom's best friend, Sister Taylor (a college-educated teacher I'd known since birth), who made the pitch to me at the start of my sophomore year. She boasted about all the great things this program would do for me, and the more she talked about it, the more excited I was to join. Ever since I was about twelve years old, I had a dream of becoming a lawyer similar to Perry Mason; I would prosecute the bad guy and preserve justice for all. I was hooked on watching all sorts of different law and crime TV shows, and I loved how the lawyer saved the day and won the case at the end of each episode. I had this *LA Law* mindset in my head, one in which I'd picture myself in court, arguing my client's case and winning at the end of the day. I knew I was going to go to college, and Upward Bound felt like the next step I needed to take to get there. It would help me get a better idea of what college would even look like, yes, but I had no idea how much it would help me realize what I wanted in my life. I applied, and Sister Taylor helped me get accepted into the program.

Upward Bound provided me with some of the most pivotal experiences I had growing up. For one thing, it helped me better understand my future and my desire to become more independent. I didn't want to continuously be underneath the ever-growing shadow of my siblings, and I didn't want to constantly be under the tutelage of my parents. I was always the baby, their miracle baby, constantly treated like a child who always needed her parents' consent to do anything because they didn't trust her. It was exhausting, and I didn't even realize it until I was allowed some degree of independence.

This was also a transformative experience that allowed me to open up more with different people. I was able to meet people from all across Nevada and California, people from all walks of life, and I got to know them and their stories. I was already outgoing when I was with my friends in our own circles, but getting to know so many more people who were all like me and in this program together helped push my boundaries. It was like an eggshell around my shelteredness was starting to crack. I started to really enjoy my high school years, and the next thing I knew, I was being invited out and hanging out with more people. It was gratifying to have these experiences, to feel like I started to belong somewhere, to know there was a pathway forward for me. Even if I didn't have all the pieces yet, I at least felt like I was starting to build toward something.

Those feelings and growth continued over the summer with what Upward Bound dubbed their Summer Games. It was an Olympics-like event during which each program across Nevada and California had the opportunity to compete in various activities for prizes and glory. For two weeks, program participants stayed on a select college campus in California, where we had a chance to mingle and have some fun in the sun. This was my first chance to get away from home, and it was like a dream come true. No parents, no relatives, just kids my age with the common goal of winning a gold medal in track and field and in bowling.

What made it such a great experience was that my mom trusted this program so much that she released her fears of my traveling alone and gave me a chance to thoroughly enjoy the experience. For the first time, I felt like I could go somewhere without having to worry about asking for permission or being out too late somewhere. It was like getting behind the wheel of a car for the first time by yourself without someone constantly making comments about your driving. It was a breath of fresh air, and I took full advantage of it.

That summer was also when I met my first real crush, my first real interest in a girl, Jamie. We met at a sponsored event and started talking. Let's be real, I told a joke and she laughed. It broke the ice, and I was smitten. At first it seemed like I had made another friend; similar experiences and trying to figure out our places in the world led us to join the program. But as the summer progressed, we grew closer and closer, cheering each other on when we were playing our own sports or games. Any chance we got, we were next to each other, and we cried when we had to leave each other. Before I knew it, we were holding hands and talking about the future and our plans, and she told me about her college goals and the career she wanted to build for herself. I was awestruck by her and inspired by her vision for the future.

The more we talked, the deeper our bond grew. It was an intimacy on an emotional level, one I'd never felt with another girl before and in a way that felt deeper than anything I'd experienced. I didn't know what love felt like at the time, and I don't even know whether this could be fully considered love, but there was a feeling of emotional love, a care for each other that was neither romantic nor sexual, one that was formed from the connections we made with each other and the openness we had by being together.

At times, being together awakened me as every feeling and emotion about my sexuality began to peak. But I kept those feelings tightly guarded and under lock and key. Every bit of hope and fear I'd been holding onto about what I'd felt from such an early age, from hours and even days of bigotry from church to all the tightly buried feelings I had about other girls, felt like it was starting to come undone. I was slowly beginning to accept that I was gay.

My only understanding of what "gay" meant was from what my dad had told me when I was in sixth grade. He was the referee for the recreation center for Reno's park, and I would accompany him sometimes. It was fun to be out with him and learn about whatever game he was the referee for that day. For me, though, I was in absolute heaven when we'd go there and find a bunch of women playing softball. I watched in awe until my dad would come up and say "You know these women are different."

I had no idea what he was talking about. "No," I said. "What do you mean?"

"Well, you know, you don't see a lot of guys here."

"Okay . . .?" It was as if he expected me to pick up the answer from his cryptic language.

"Oh, I mean they're gay."

That was it. He didn't elaborate on what that even meant, and I had to pick it up from context clues. I saw couples together after they finished playing, and I was attracted to that, to the companionship they had from being together. That's what I understood as "gay": committing to a same-sex partner and being together with one another emotionally.

I didn't even think of myself as a gay until four years after my experience with Jamie. She brought everything I'd been feeling to the forefront of my mind. There was no denying it anymore, and there was no way I could put my own feelings back in the closet. In a way, Jamie allowed me to feel comfortable enough with myself to accept what I knew all along. Now I had to figure out what it all meant.

I left that summer with a lot on my mind. Because Jamie lived in California, we had only the summer to get close to each other, and without the internet or even a pager, we weren't able to keep in touch. Much like with Kelly, things fizzled out after the summer, and it left a hole in me. I was finally able to develop an emotional relationship with another girl, and to acknowledge that my sexuality wasn't just about sex opened my mind to what having a full relationship like this would mean to me. All of that felt like it was stripped away when the summer ended.

It was heartbreaking that I couldn't be with her anymore, but in the long run it was probably for the best. She unlocked a lot of who I am today, and being intimate with her was an incredible experience, but would I really want to spend the rest of my life with this person? No, I wouldn't. Being ready to fall in love with the first girl I felt something real with is the type of feeling I had when I was a kid, and it's what I understood as a relationship. In reality, if we had continued to see each other, my life would've gone in a very different direction, but at the time I didn't know whether I'd ever feel this same connection again. Finding other queer people in the '80s wasn't the easiest thing to do, as we all seemed to be in the proverbial closet.

Once Jamie and I parted ways, I realized that the floodgates had been opened and that there wasn't any way I could shut down my emotions. Now I just needed to find a girl. But who?

Realization and Acceptance, Winter 1987

The following year, I opted to try out for the volleyball team. It was something new that I hadn't done before, and I had a friend who went with me for tryouts. It was when I was walking into the gym that I saw my butch Cindy Crawford. She had just been hired to become the latest volleyball coach and was the woman of my dreams. She had long, dark, feathered hair, a bit of a muscular build, and the deepest blue eyes that washed over me like a wave. To my young gay eyes, everything she did felt like it was done with grace and beauty.

She could do no wrong, and I instantly had a crush on her. Me being on the team didn't pan out, but I expressed enough interest in wanting to be a part of the team that they positioned me as the scorekeeper. It was a nice enough gesture, but I was just glad I could still be close to my coach.

The more practices I went to, the more my feelings for her went beyond just a high school crush. She was openly gay, and only with a select few spoke openly yet privately about her partner. I was one of the chosen few, which was unfortunate because my girl crush was hard and I kept fantasizing about ways to wrestle her away and make her my own. She was the first openly gay woman I'd ever known, and my curiosity often got the better of me. I asked her about her life and journey whenever I got the chance, and after asking so much about her life, it kind of became obvious why I was asking, at least to me. I was falling in love, but I was careful not to show it. Discreetly, I left unsigned love notes topped with a red rose, which showed I meant business with these unrequited gestures. This would soon be my calling card for the future, but at least by the time I reached adulthood the feelings were (hopefully) reciprocated.

Over time, my coach became like a gay mentor to me. There was no way I could be open and out like her, but she gave me that safe space I needed to talk about my experiences and what I was feeling. She told me about her experiences before coming out and what it was like being in a relationship, and I soaked it all up like a sponge. It was great to hear and learn from her, but there was a flip side: She was how I learned about discrimination, and being openly gay in the '80s was about as glamorous as you'd expect. She faced a lot of hate in her day-to-day life, whether it was people giving her looks or spewing verbal, sometimes physical hatred toward her. In the years before Ellen DeGeneres rocked the TV world to its core by reminding us that gay people exist everywhere and starting a wave of influential queer people coming out, no one talked about their sexuality. Everything was kept under wraps, and even if someone presented as queer, no one commented about it or brought it into the light because no one liked to talk about it.

My coach explained her experiences to me not in an optimistic or nihilistic way but in a matter-of-fact way, one that was like, "This is our reality right now, and it's important to recognize what it is to try to live within it." Her being open about queer relationships was an open defiance of the status quo, and I couldn't help but feel inspired by her and her words. Yes, things were hard, but seeing an openly gay woman and learning from her gave me hope that one day maybe I could be the same. Maybe in the future I could help tell other queer people it's okay to be who you are, even in the face of hate and people who'd rather pretend and bury any thought about sexuality. Maybe one day I'd get around to writing a book or something.

My volleyball coach was the first queer person I could really connect with, but that quickly expanded afterward. It was almost as if my starting to internally embrace my sexuality allowed me to start making other queer connections. Soon after starting to talk with my coach, I came out to two of my friends, Steven and Lyn, who came out to me at the same time. We had known one another since meeting in driver's ed class and clowning around, and we formed fast friendships. Ironically, the three of us never spent time together in one room, but both of them were crucial supports for me during that time.

Surprisingly enough for the time, coming out to them was pretty casual. For Steven, I was over at his house, and we were sitting on the couch watching MTV when he said he had a crush on someone. It felt out of nowhere, but I asked who, and he said one of the guys who was playing in the music video. I took it in and was like, "Oh! You know I have a crush on someone too, my oft-mentioned crush on Cindy Crawford." And that was that. There was no big moment when I felt tense about saying it, and Steven made me feel invited to talk about it. From that point on, he was someone I could go to, to talk about what I was feeling. He was another safe person I could reach out to and have the difficult conversations I felt I couldn't have with anyone else, and in turn he felt the same way. We were both learning and growing together. Neither of us had any idea where any of this would lead, but we looked past high school toward what was next and how we were going to get there. Those were questions that lingered in my mind.

My coming out to Lyn was done in a similar nonchalant way. It was during a random conversation we were having about some of our classmates, and the way she was talking about some of the girls probably should've clued me in. But in conversation she just said, "Yeah, I like girls," and my response was, "Oh! So do I."

And that was the extent of my coming-out story, until years later when I came out to my parents. That, too, was not very long or elaborate. As with Steven, it was a mutual understanding of who we each were and feeling safe with one another.

After my coming out to Lyn, our friendship became deeper. There was no romantic attraction between us, but we continued to push each other to be more authentic. Our friendship grew quickly, and she became another person I could truly confide in. One of few, unfortunately.

Besides Lyn, Steven, and my volleyball coach, I had no one I felt comfortable enough talking to about what it was like to be queer. In the '80s, few people talked about sex, let alone sexuality. We all needed to rebel against our parents and feel more grown up than we actually were, something we were all experiencing and could relate to in school, but the experience of being queer was something that had to be kept secret. Between Lyn, Steven, and me, none of us could wrap our heads around being open about our sexuality. You either stayed in the closet or faced the repercussions of your friends and family and constantly being verbally or physically harassed.

It gets exhausting having to go through every day putting on a hetero mask and pretending like there isn't something you're holding deep inside you, playing a role just to avoid any sort of retaliation, slipping under the radar to avoid constantly being called slurs in school. You learn to say things only in private, and you feel guarded when people ask about things such as relationships and the future. It's an extremely lonely feeling, like being in a room full of people yet still sitting alone. Everyone is going about their conversations like normal, and you're left wondering who's safe to talk to.

Confiding in Steven and Lyn was a breath of fresh air. I was, and still am, grateful to the two of them and the support they gave me during those high school years. I still felt a sense of being alone in a crowded room, but I at least felt safe to talk with two people in said room. It was invigorating to have two people in my life who were gay and expressed their sexuality to me. It allowed me the opportunity to be more open around them about how I was feeling and what I was thinking. It was like a weight being lifted off my shoulders, and I was able to support both of them as well. We were able to fully express ourselves in those moments, and though they were few and far in between, they helped me navigate my own understanding of myself through those years.

We kept things hidden pretty well, and none of us thought about the possibility of expressing ourselves so openly, at least until prom happened. The first sign of self-awareness and a bit of defiance showed up at our senior prom, when Lyn showed up in a full tuxedo. She hadn't told anyone (including myself) she was going to do it, and everyone who saw her was shocked, myself floored. The irony of the situation showed the times. Not one person caused a commotion over it, though for the most part it was the talk of the event. People even took pictures and complimented her style. Could it have been that folks knew she was gay, or simply that she had the guts to just be herself? We may never know, but that night Lyn became the coolest closeted gay person in Reno (in my humble opinion).

Even by bringing her faux boyfriend with her, Lyn demonstrated something that went beyond being just a tomboy. To me it was awesome to see her defy gender norms and express herself in that way, to be authentic in her clothes without having to name the reasons behind it, not that she could be completely honest if people asked. But it was as if I were playing both sides. On one hand I was just as stunned as everyone else seeing her show up in a tux, but I knew the reasons behind her doing it. I knew she was openly expressing her sexuality in a bold way, and since only the two of us had that knowledge, it was like me silently telling her "I see you" while also pretending I had no idea why she would do something so out there.

It wasn't until afterward that Lyn told me she was terrified the entire time, afraid of anyone saying anything and what she would do in response. Luckily, nothing happened that night and we all had a good time, but I couldn't imagine what would've happened if I were in her shoes. I would've loved to have worn a tux since I hate dressing up, but I could imagine the panic I would've felt even bringing up the idea to my parents and the barrage of questions from family about why I'd want to do this. I could almost hear my mom saying to me, "Wouldn't you rather wear a dress?" and I could imagine their disapproval and most likely outright refusal to support me in sporting a tux. It was an unthinkable idea to me, but seeing Lyn rock it that night redefined what I thought was possible. I imagine she blazed a trail for other kids to express themselves authentically in that school, whether through how they chose to dress or who they wanted to bring to prom.

About a month later, I knew I needed to make some kind of change. I needed to be freer. My relationship with Manny had changed. We'd been together for over two years at this point and gotten pretty close, but something felt different. I couldn't envision a future with him as I began to explore my sexuality. Our relationship was more friendly than romantic, and an innocent relationship at that. We'd go out for pizza and spend time on the couch with each other watching TV. It lacked the intimacy I needed in a relationship, and, ironically, being with him helped me realize I could not be a girlfriend to a boyfriend. I needed to end things if I was going to figure out what I needed in the future from a partner.

I didn't really know how to go about it, and it didn't end well. I thought that the faster I ended the conversation, the easier it would be, but I learned really quickly that this wasn't a great way to handle situations like these. It sucked that he left hurt, and I felt terrible about hurting him and losing a childhood friend, but at the same time it was a freeing feeling. After breaking up with him, I felt like I could breathe again. I wasn't tied to anyone, and I was free to explore a side of me I felt like I'd never been able to before. Albeit it was within the bounds of staying in the closet, but still. It was more than I had before.

❦ ❦ ❦

Months later, I got the chance to explore more of myself during the next session of Upward Bound. Moving out of my junior year and into my senior year, I went away for the summer to again be a part of the program, only this time as a junior coordinator. It was a great time for me. I could get out for the summer, and I was able to feel some sense of independence on the campus.

I arrived at the dorms before anyone else, or at least I thought I did. There was one other girl there, one I had a crush on from the last time we were both in the program. We instantly recognized each other and started talking, catching up on what had happened in the year prior, but we started to move closer to one another. I don't know whether she had a really good gaydar, but the chemistry in the room was there, and the next thing I knew we were in bed together. It felt like it happened so fast. It was beyond awkward pretending as though nothing had happened when others began to arrive in their respective rooms.

That moment awakened so many things inside me about who I was and what I wanted. almost like a confirmation that everything I'd been thinking in my head was real. The intimacy, the passion, the desire . . . all of it. It wasn't just what I wanted but what I needed in life. I needed a friend, a lover, a girlfriend to make me always feel the way I did that day.

That experience became a closely guarded memory for both of us. Nothing more ever came from it, and I'm kind of glad nothing did. I was able to explore more of what I wanted without having to feel like I was obligated or tied down with this girl in any way. We went on through the program as if nothing had ever happened and we were just two friends, and our moment together was something I didn't feel comfortable sharing with anyone but Lyn. But that experience was freeing. Even though it was only for a moment in the middle of summer, it made me feel like I could let down my guard, that I could fully be myself with another woman, that who I was, was more than enough.

However that moment also left me with an uncomfortable feeling because I wasn't able to fully be myself afterward. Having this experience was great, but there was a big question mark when it ended, like whether there was going to be something to follow it. Now what? What happens now? What is supposed to happen now? Neither Lyn nor I had the answer to those questions. All we could do was just keep going through high school, hold these memories close to our hearts, and hope it happened again.

It also left me with a feeling of wanting to be more open about this. I wish I could've been able to share my life without having to fear what other people would say. Why should my experiences be hidden when other people could say them loudly and proudly without any consequence? Why were my thoughts and feelings treated as less than just because the person I had an attraction to was the same gender as me? Why should I feel shame for the way I feel?

All these questions bubbled up within me, and all I wanted to do was scream out to the world, "This is who I am, and nothing can take this part of myself away from me."

Chapter 4

Where Is My Future?

Found Family, Summer 1988

Every day that went by left me with a feeling of wanting to be more open. Like water heating up in a kettle on a hot stove, that feeling built up within me, and I could hear my soul screaming out from within to come out to more people around me.

Coming out is never an easy thing to do. There are so many variables to consider when trying to figure out who's safe, who'll have a favorable reaction, and how differently someone might think of me if I do come out to them. Trying to figure out who was safe to come out to was particularly challenging. It's hard to start talking about how someone might feel about someone else being gay without that being a dead giveaway, especially since no one talked about being gay and there wasn't anyone to point to and ask, "What was it like to be with Stacy? Does the carpet match the drapes?" It's a crass example but one widely discussed at that time.

The idea of coming out to my family never felt like an option given comments my dad had made to me about queer people, and all the knowledge I had about sexuality was based on society's negative reactions and the fear-mongering I experienced from those who had zero experience in the community. No one around me outside of Steven and Lyn talked about being gay, and I felt like I was forever stuck in the closet with no way out.

As I kept thinking back and forth about who might be safe to come out to, I regularly met up with my old friend Lisa from middle school. Even though the two of us went to different high schools, we'd regularly meet up over the year, especially during the summer when we'd spend just about every day together until my freshman year of college and playing tennis. It was our way of staying connected with each other even though we had neither the skills nor the talent of Evert or Navratilova. She picked me up to go play one day, and something within me told me I needed to come out to her. I felt like she was the one person I could come out to at the time. She was my best friend, and the one friend I'd known the longest. If there was one straight person I felt even remotely comfortable holding my secret at the time, it was her.

Even though I knew it was what I needed and wanted to do, the buildup to saying it was nerve-racking. What was her reaction going to be? Would our friendship end when I told her who I was? These questions swirled around in my head until I finally said something.

There wasn't any grand way of saying it, at least none I could come up with at the moment, but in the middle of a tense love–love (0–0) tiebreaker, I felt it was finally a good time to tell her that I love other women. "Hey Lisa!" I yelled across the tennis court. "Let's take a break from the intensity of the game," I remarked sarcastically. She relented, as she knew she was leading the match.

"What's up?" she asked pensively.

I took a gulp and replied, "Well, I've been wanting to share this with you for a while, but I am gay."

The few seconds before her reaction felt like an eternity of waiting to see whether I still had a best friend.

She smiled and said, "I'm proud of you for sharing that with me."

Her response gave me a feeling of connection, especially given the difficulty I thought would come from my admission. She was one of the people who got it. Her response was nonjudgmental and loving, just as a friend's should be.

Afterward, we proceeded to have a longer conversation about what all of this meant, and at the end of it she asked if I was okay. It was the reverse of what I expected; *I* should've been the one to ask if *she* was okay at the end of it, considering what I'd told her. "I'm better now," I said.

The conversation ended with a hug, and we quickly went back to our match. I think she won that day, although I was the winner of a true friend and tennis partner.

From that point on, the bond between us deepened. She became one of the few people who kept my secret, and I trusted her with it. Conversations between us intensified, and we became more like sisters. In Lisa I found a sister who gave me the support, encouragement, and friendship I longed to have with my biological sister. We're still friends to this day, and I cherish the time we were able to spend together and the time we made for each other.

We made sure to make the most of the rest of the summer and our last year in high school together before we went off on whatever adventure happened next. None of this resolved my fear of coming out to other people, but knowing there was at least one more person I could trust released a little bit of the pain. At this point, only three people knew who I fully was, and they became my closest confidants and found family.

Can the Future Really Be Bright? Fall 1988

Going into my senior year was bittersweet. It was the beginning of the end of the road that's paved out for all kids. Everyone around me knew exactly what they were going to do when they graduated. Just about everyone was going to college, with the exception of one or two kids who chose to go into the military. I was the kid who was left out, with no real idea of what I should do. There wasn't a predetermined road map to follow anymore. *Now what?* was a question that had been in my mind since I started high school, and I'd have to answer it eventually.

I knew I wanted to go to college, but it was a matter of which college I'd go to and whether I could even get in. During my time in high school, I wasn't the most studious person; I was thoroughly enjoying my senior year and basking in the time I had left. Yes, I was part of a program that prepared me for college, but that didn't necessarily prepare me to take tests and excel enough to get into a big-name school. I was a B- to C-average student, and I didn't perform exceedingly well on any of the standardized tests that grant admission into college. College felt like where I should go, but the idea of getting there felt so far away from any reality I could conceive.

Mom could see the struggle I was going through but didn't know how to help. As the perceived spoiled third child, I was graced with not being pushed as hard to go to a prestigious college as my siblings, but I was told I should think about going to a trade school (eye roll). In all honesty, it was the worst idea. I was not trade school material. I wanted to be a lawyer, and my aspirations were high even if my grades didn't match those aspirations. I felt confused and hopeless. I had all this preparation about what it would be like to get into college, but I had no pathway to get there.

At the high school I went to, every student was required to take a career aptitude test that asked about their futures, such as what we aspired to do. My test results clearly established that I was college material. Another requirement was that we were all assigned to guidance counselors at the beginning of our sophomore year to help us prepare for our futures. I didn't actually see my counselor until my junior year of high school, when I felt the dread of the future coming over me.

At the start of my junior year, I gathered the courage to talk to Mrs. Bond her about my future. As I stepped into her office, she immediately responded with, "Oh, you finally showed up."

I laughed at her backhanded comment, then opened up to her about my family's history with college, including the fact that my siblings had graduated from Stanford and Pepperdine, respectively. I also told her that my mother clearly wasn't aware of my collegial strengths or the aptitude test and felt I was more suited for trade school.

I expected Ms. Bond to agree with my mom, but after looking at my aptitude test she said that I was college material, I just wasn't applying myself. That was the first time I heard those words.

We spent the next thirty minutes going over potential colleges given my test scores and abilities, and we came up with two different schools. One was a state college in Colorado, and the other was a college in Vermont focused on liberal arts, which was a big interest for me. She not only helped reignite my desire to try to apply to colleges again but also guided me through the process, telling me which forms I needed to fill out. By providing actual guidance on what I needed to do, Mrs. Bond put me back on the path to college, and I soon set my sights on the possibilities I had in front of me, keeping my thoughts about these colleges in my head until my senior year.

The more time went on, the more I had to ask myself, *If I want to get into a college, what is the path going to look like for me?* I knew

I needed to get out of the house and start exploring who I was, so eventually I applied to both colleges. It wasn't until months later that I got any notices about either. It was close to my graduation when I finally got two letters back. I didn't get into the school in Colorado, but Vermont was willing to give me a chance, and I received a tentative acceptance, which thrilled me.

I thought about going out of state like my siblings had done before me, but without any scholarship or grant money to get me there, it was more a dream than a reality. My parents weren't able to help much either, given how much it costs to go to school out of state, and taking out a loan was a huge taboo for the time. Much to my sadness, my parents informed me that if they had the money, they would help me, but they didn't.

I felt despondent and frustrated. For the first time in my life I'd committed to leaving Reno and finding my own path, but I was suddenly stopped in my tracks by lack of funds. For a beautiful two months, I envisioned myself stepping foot on campus and finally having a chance to be my own person. But without any real financial means of getting to Vermont, let alone living there and attending school, it was more of a pipe dream. Still, the thought of going to a college remained at the front of my mind.

While all this was happening, the huge relationship gap between me and my parents, one that began when I started high school, seemed to be growing. I so desperately wanted to be on my own and away from constant supervision, away from the constant concern about me being out on my own. I argued with my mom about why I couldn't stay overnight at a friend's house. Why was I constantly coddled as if I were a five-year-old kid who was gullible enough to take candy from a stranger's truck? Why me? Because I'm the youngest out of three? Because I nearly died as a baby? Why was I treated so differently than my siblings?

Today, I completely understand why my mom was so protective. I've come to realize that I would be equally protective given I'd never want anything to happen to my child. With age comes wisdom, and my younger self couldn't see or understand that.

The straw that broke the camel's back came the night of my senior skit. The idea was a play on *The Breakfast Club* meets *The Wizard of Oz*, combining the two movies together, and I was playing the Cowardly Lion. My friends and I joined the skit and were excited for the moment we would debut the show; it was one of the last big school events that brought us all together as a senior class. I made sure to tell my parents the time it was happening, and I wanted to make sure they had all the information about it. They even helped me buy a lion costume for the skit, and I couldn't wait to perform for them. I was excited for them to have a proud parent moment. That moment never came.

I stepped out on stage to perform as the mighty yet Cowardly Lion. I was acting out on stage, giving it my all, enjoying the moment of this final high school event. I couldn't see anyone in the audience, but I felt for sure my parents were out there, proud as could be. It wasn't until the curtain call, when all the lights came up and my eyes were less dilated, that I could see who was in the audience. I scanned all the rows, but no. They didn't show up. As I watched as everyone else rejoice while they hugged their parents and family, I stood alone. Humiliated and angry, I was able to get a ride home.

When I got home, I exploded on my mom for their no-show. I yelled, "Everyone's parents were there, but mine were not." After a few minutes, I calmly asked, "What happened?" The tears welled in my eyes as I looked down at the kitchen floor.

"Kelli," she responded, "I had every intention of going, but you know I don't drive, and your dad had to work late. I'm sorry."

I stormed into my room, where I sat in the dark with my feelings. I knew deep in my heart that she would've been there if she could've been, but at that moment I felt very alone in the world. And being that I was eighteen, this event felt like the worst thing that could've happened to me. No excuse in the world could make up for the fact that my parents had disappointed me. And it wasn't the first time, nor would it be the last.

To be clear, both of my parents were there for me when I physically needed them, and they made sure my siblings and I were taken care of, but they were never really there for me on an emotional level. My dad wasn't around much; he'd show up for school events with my mom, but outside of that he was either busy with work or off somewhere else. As overprotective as my mother was, I felt that I couldn't confide in her and tell her what I was feeling. While I often felt her hovering over me like a fly on the wall, always watching and doing everything she could to take care of me, it's hard to talk with a fly. She seemed to have her own issues with distance, and later I learned she was dealing with my dad's unfaithfulness while struggling with her mental health. She spent hours alone in her own bedroom, reading the Bible, watching TV, or just waiting for my dad to come home. It saddened me to watch my mom living her own nightmare, alone and afraid. It seemed God was her only refuge, and I found myself staying out of the way, often feeling as if I wasn't the child they all hoped for.

Growing up, I thought that my mom's smothering of me was the way love is expressed. It became my rationale for how to love, and I often found myself expressing "love" in this manner with others, especially in relationships. Looking back on it now, I can tell how quickly that turned me toward the path to wanting my own independence yet still understanding that my parents loved me the best way they knew how. It's a struggle I still battle with to this day. Thank you, baby Jesus, for therapy.

The dream of going away to college was still on my mind, but I could never find a way to get over the hurdle that was the amount of money it would take to get there. I was floundering and trying not to think about the possibility of not going to college. As much as I would've liked to think some wish-saving miracle would save me in the end, nothing like happened. And things only got more difficult in the first week of April, days before my eighteenth birthday.

Throughout my adolescence, my grandmother was there to support me in whatever I was doing, and she kept the family together. She was one of my closest family members, the one who prayed over me when I was born. Early in my second year of high school, she suffered a stroke. It was sudden, and she was rushed to the hospital. Everyone in my family was terrified about what could happen. Luckily she was able to recover from it, but not without complications. Over time, it was like watching a slow decline. Soon after having that stroke, she needed a wheelchair in order to get around. Anytime I saw her, I could see her strength leaving her compared to the week prior. I could see she was in pain, and my heart cried out for the inevitable.

Even with all the time in the world and seeing what's happening, knowing what comes next never makes the experience any better. In her last year, my family sensed she was preparing to leave this earth, but no one could've predicted when or the catastrophic effect it would have on our family. She was our rock and my personal heroine.

It happened four days before my birthday. As much as my family and I tried to prepare for it, the phone call came early on a sad Thursday morning. My dad got the call, and he woke me up to tell me what happened. Thankfully, he also called the school and got me the day off to process it. We were devastated, and it took us a while to fully comprehend she was gone. All of us were heartbroken and broke down. I so desperately wanted her to make it to my high school graduation and see me proudly accepting my diploma, to see me moving on to the next part of my life, to show her that all the investments she made in me, whether financial, emotional, or spiritual, were worth it.

My grandmother's death left a hole in the family, one that was never filled by anyone else. In the days after she passed, I tried to think to myself, *At least she's no longer in pain. She's no longer suffering just to live.* With everything else that was happening, I tried to suppress the sadness, anguish, and pain losing her caused, but I kept one thought close to my heart: Above all, out of all of my family members, she would've loved me if I'd come out to her. I held that thought through graduation.

Come and Gone, Summer 1989

With graduation looming around the corner, I needed to figure out some plan for after high school. At the last minute and with my dad's assistance, I was accepted into the University of Nevada, Reno (UNR). A huge weight came off not only my shoulders but also those of my parents, who'd been so worried thinking I wasn't going to go to college. UNR definitely wasn't my first choice, given that it was only about five to ten minutes away from my parents, but at least it was out of their house.

Graduation day came and I proudly accepted my diploma, celebrating the day with my parents and family. That night, Lyn and I were ready to put our plans together to spend the night celebrating our independence. Miraculously, when I told my mom I was going to be over at Lyn's for the night, she didn't say anything. Maybe she finally loosened her hold on me because it was graduation. Regardless, I was ecstatic and quickly got dressed in my best butch outfit for a summer in 1989: a pair of jeans and a T-shirt.

After eighteen years of lived experience, Lyn and I thought we were adults and could do whatever we wanted. At first I thought it was just going to be the two of us since her parents were around, but I was pleasantly surprised when she told me she had invited two older women who were family friends. Looking back, it's clear they were a lesbian couple, but at that time either my gaydar was on hiatus or the antenna was a bit bent. Whatever the reason, it didn't dawn on me that this was yet another life-changing experience.

Lyn picked me up, and we were off to her house to meet with the couple. We started the night having pizza and watching my first lesbian movie, *Desert Hearts*, an '80s movie filmed in and around Reno. The movie ends with the main characters going their separate directions, but something ignited in me when it came to the understanding of "lesbian love." I wanted it! I needed it! But I had no idea how to get it.

Lyn and I were separated with these two women in between us, and we were all chatting with each other, everyone seeming jovial and having a good time. Halfway through the movie, Lyn and one of the women left the room and went to some other part of the house, leaving me with the other woman. We started talking for a bit and she had her hand on my knee. In my head I was just awestruck, thinking, *What is happening and what's about to happen?* The next thing I knew, we were kissing. Nothing else happened, no sex or any physical contact other than kissing, yet I was smitten. All I could think about the entire time was, *Holy shit, I want to do this all the time.* It was almost a romanticized version of lesbianism. The level of intimacy in kissing another woman who wants to kiss another woman was something I'd only dreamed about, and with someone who's confident in who they are, knows what they want, and isn't going to hide themselves outside the protection of a living room. I wanted to have that feeling all the time.

After Lyn and the other woman came back from the other room, we all decided to go out to dinner. We made small talk with each other throughout the night, and the couple shared that they were in an open relationship. This sentiment oddly reassured me that I wasn't stepping over any boundaries set by the two of them. It was a comforting feeling being all together and enjoying each other's company.

When we got back from dinner, they ended up leaving, and the woman I'd been with gave me a kiss goodnight. It all felt like a dream, and I could barely believe that it happened.

The next day and evening, we did normal things together (shopping at the mall, going to another movie, and eating more pizza), and the day after that, life kept moving on. It felt so weird to think about, and it does even now. As though it were a dream, I never saw either of those women again. It was like a fateful moment in a cheesy Hallmark Christmas movie except instead of teaching me the meaning of Christmas, they taught me the complexity of being a lesbian, and relationships for that matter.

Lyn and I never really talked about that night other than very surface-level conversations way later in our lives. We mostly acknowledged that it definitely happened and nothing more, like a gentle head nod saying, "Nope, you did not dream what happened." The night overall might have been simplistic—watching a movie, eating pizza, making out—but for me it was magical and dizzying all in one. It confirmed exactly what I knew was in my heart all this time; I just finally had my first moment of fully realizing it: *I am gay and would like more of this.*

My idea of what my life would be like going forward was complicated because I didn't know what my life was going to be like from moment to moment every day. I didn't have these two women who came as swiftly into my life as they exited it to be guides for how to be gay. But meeting both of them changed what being gay meant for me. It confirmed that an intimate, romantic relationship with a woman was possible, and the possibility of living freely and openly opened my eyes to the idea that maybe someday I, too, wouldn't have to hide myself out of fear of retaliation. Maybe someday I'd be in a relationship. Maybe one day I'd write a book or something that will help show young lesbians it's okay to be who they are and be what they want to be.

It seems like such a silly thing to think about in hindsight, but no one walks you through what it's like to be a lesbian or encourages you to be yourself, which I needed at the time. Had I not been fearful of what would've happened, I would've come out earlier, but that's part of the period I grew up in. I had to figure out how to move forward on my own, how to define myself with no guidance, and boy did I need guidance early on in college.

Every College Freshman Just Wants to Have Fun, Fall 1989

Attending college locally felt similar to spending another summer with Upward Bound, which was being held on the campus of UNR. After a day of consideration, I decided to live on campus. The difference was, since I'd already spent months in the building and the dorms and already knew the area, I was now a college student.

I completely relished those first couple of days alone. It was the first time I could finally say I was free, free to be on my own and make my own decisions for myself. It felt like all the shackles had fallen off and I was finally free to do, well, anything! Anything I set my mind to I could do, and there wasn't anyone to tell me no, no one to tell me that I was staying out too late, that I couldn't go over to a friend's house, or that I couldn't eat only a bowl of ramen for the day. My ambition to do anything and everything was high, and I even hosted a blaxploitation "film festival" in my dorm room. True independence was something I relished, even if the college was only a little over five minutes away from my parents.

The first night of orientation, the freshmen were introduced to all the things the campus offered, from the student center to the lecture halls. There was also a showcase for all the sororities and fraternities on campus you could join. Even though I was never really sorority material, I was always happy to talk with the sisters and get invitations to their parties, especially since they made no effort to hide the alcohol.

My mind was swimming with ideas and plans about what I was going to do and which party I was going to for the week, and I gave little to no thought about what I was going to do in terms of my education. I started out as a psychology major for reasons that are beyond even me. Was I thinking I was going to be a psychologist or therapist? Hell no, but it seemed like the most appealing option when I had no idea what major I should pick. I still had the idea in my head that I was going to go to law school and be a lawyer by the time I was thirty. The education it took to get to law school didn't matter to me at the time, a point I'm still kicking myself for forty years later.

My lack of discipline in high school wasn't made any better by my newfound freedom. I was mostly an average student in high school, and that only got worse in college. All I wanted to do was focus on living the best college life and finding out what that meant. I was lost in a haze, constantly asking myself, *Who am I?* I thought the more I experienced, the more I did, the closer I'd get to finding out the answer. As it turns out, you don't really get to understand who you are from the bottom of a red Solo cup. Not that I would've listened to that bit of advice at the time anyway.

For a college freshman, getting to that answer mostly means partying a lot and doing all the things they couldn't before. I made fast friends with other people in my classes, and my ears would perk up the minute I heard my friends mention they were going to a party or something similar. I wanted to be involved in everything that wasn't studying for my classes.

Ironically enough, I held onto the idyllic dream of getting out of Reno and going to a prestigious college. I wanted to get out and explore the world, and I felt like I couldn't create an identity in Reno; I couldn't begin to shape myself as a person, let alone as a gay woman. My golden ticket was to get into the University of California, Los Angeles (UCLA).

My fascination with the LA lifestyle began in my youth. I created an idyllic vision of what LA was from when I spent time there with my family or went to visit my sister in the summer. Everything there felt exciting, and staying in Malibu for my sister's graduation only grew my fascination with LA. It felt like its own world, with celebrities, money, and all sorts of things I'd never seen before. It felt like a city where I could start being me, and UCLA, in the posh neighborhood of Brentwood, was in the heart of it.

My dream of going to UCLA stems from seeing both my siblings graduate from prestigious colleges. *When I graduate from UCLA, I'll join them in this hall of prestige*, I imagined in my head, finally being equal to both of them and no longer the white sheep of the family. They applied themselves and graduated with honors, while I was struggling not only with not flunking out of UNR but with a feeling of being "abnormal." And not just because I was gay but because I was the only one in the family with a physical disability, which meant I had to constantly get special accommodations from my teachers. That made the differences between me and my siblings that much more apparent, but I still believed I would get into UCLA and turn everything around.

I talked constantly about going to UCLA, like it was a thing that had already happened before I even applied. I even spent a good amount of time wearing UCLA gear to get me in the spirit of being a Bruin, as if it would manifest the acceptance letter coming to my mailbox and everything would take off from there. I felt like I'd made it to the top of the mountain and had all the stars in front of me, infinite choices, and I was determined to make it to LA.

As it turns out, barely passing grades in your first semester doesn't make for a good application to a renowned university. My application, much to my eighteen-year-old self's surprise, was denied. If I was in my shoes with what I know now, I would've taken this as a sign that I needed to buckle down and start focusing on my grades and finish my degree at UNR before continuing with my ideal vision of what I saw for my future. Instead, I committed to the idea of going to LA and figuring it out when I got there.

I was devastated when I got the rejection letter, but I wasn't going to let that stop me. Even if it took multiple times, I was not going to stop trying. I still wanted to fulfill my dream of being a lawyer by the time I was thirty, and with tunnel vision I did anything I could to get out of Reno. I kept thinking, *When I get to LA, I'll have so much more to figure out and explore, and everything will really come together.* So I focused hard on having as much fun as possible, enjoying my newfound freedom and making a ton of decisions I regret, just like many college freshmen.

With the summer approaching, I really had nothing better to do than continue what I was already doing, except now there weren't any tests coming up.

Hazy Shade of Summer, 1990

In May, I returned to my parents' house, where I proceeded to spend the next three months attending summer school and working. I had secured a position at UNR as a summer intern with Upward Bound, which I loved more than life itself. I took every chance I had to hang with my friends, and I found myself invited to party after party, which was a complete contrast to my high school social calendar. Throughout the summer, Steven and another friend hosted house parties and would invite tons of people from around town and around the area, whether they were his friends or friends of friends. There was always something happening at that house.

One night I hung out with Steven's new friends, watching a bootleg copy of a Mickey Rourke film called *Johnny Handsome*. We were all drinking wine coolers and having a great night, then suddenly a gorgeous girl appeared out of nowhere. From the minute I saw her I couldn't stop gazing. She had short blonde hair, blue eyes, a slightly muscular build, and all the confidence in the world walking into the room. I was instantly hooked, but I tried to be as discreet about it as possible. I had no way of knowing whether she was gay or would even be interested in me.

I tried to keep calm and cool as she entered the room. As we all started talking about the movie and each other, I kept trying to get a read on her, hoping I had some semblance of a gaydar working correctly, even though the term didn't even exist back then. I gave a ton of side glances and tried to jump into the conversation when she was talking with the group. After much investigation from Steven (mostly), I learned she was a summer worker for a friend's landscaping business and that her name was Jade.

The energy between me and Jade from our introduction was electric, and we ended up talking alone on a two-person bean bag in a romantic corner of the living room. I probably made some joke or something and got her interest, but next thing I knew we were making out. Everything felt right in that moment. After what felt like decades, I was finally able to freely be myself. We moved to the back of her car, almost as classy as a Best Western, where we continued to caress one another in ways that made me feel loved, wanted, and safe. With each kiss, our bodies exploded with glee and excitement, and I felt sexually free to explore this moment without fearing whether what I was doing was right or wrong or worrying whether someone might see.

I don't know how she felt or whether she had been hiding like me, but something brought the two of us together that night, and it was as if it was meant to be. It may have been only a moment, but it was one of the most impactful moments I ever had as a young gay woman.

We ended up parting ways that night but made plans to see each other again the next day. A couple of friends had invited us to a small get-together, but we ditched them and ended up spending the entire day together. We went to the mall, saw a movie, and even had a picnic. It felt so right to be with her, and I caught huge feelings for her in the first two days I knew her. Thankfully I had already planned on moving to LA, otherwise I don't doubt that I would've dropped everything in my life to go with her wherever she wanted. I was beyond smitten. We spent just about every day that summer together. Whether we were at a party house or finding our own adventures throughout the city and beyond, we were attached at the hip whenever we went, and it felt good.

Jade was my first real semblance of what having a girlfriend would be like. With Manny or Kelly, the missing ingredient was everything I felt when I was with Jade. I felt complete when I was in her arms, and I began to experience a love for someone who I believed in my heart had also been searching for years. She filled me with endless joy, and we constantly expressed our love for each other by buying each other gifts. She bought me a heart-shaped locket, and in return I bought her a silver bracelet, a declaration of our summer love for each other. Those gifts meant that when the summer was over and I went away to LA, we hoped to see each other again, that my leaving didn't mean the end of us. They were promises that we'd stay together. We both knew the day I had to leave was approaching, but with the promise bracelet, I held onto the hope we'd still be together again after college and over the summers.

Well, like all good things, even this had to reach a climactic end. It was late August, and the day for my flight to LA had unfortunately arrived. After Jade picked me up, she drove us over to the party house, where we spent some quiet time together. I wanted every minute, and I dreaded seeing the clock wind down. I tried to take in everything I was feeling. I didn't know when we'd see each other again.

Eventually the hour came and the bell rang. I couldn't put off leaving any longer. Jade drove me back to my house, but it didn't feel right to end things right there in that car, nor to know that these were my final moments with her for at least a year. I couldn't bear it and invited her into my house. She was hesitant since she knew the situation with my parents, but I was insistent, hoping to get as much time with her as I could. Plus, my parents weren't home at the time, so I knew things would be okay. Hell, even if they did come home, what's the worst that would happen? I'd say, "This is my friend," and that would be the end of it. Or so I thought.

As we walked into my family home, I started to give Jade a brief tour, showing her all the different rooms and knickknacks we had around the house that held a memory. Then we made our way to my parents' bedroom. I don't know what compelled either of us, I think we both wanted to savor the moment, but we started making out. In my parents' bedroom. Mistake number one. And as things kept going, we ended up making our way toward their bed. Mistake number two.

I didn't even consider what could happen. I was so wrapped up in her that I didn't hear the sound of the door opening. It closed as quickly as it opened, but the person who opened it didn't have the same grace for closing it. The sound of a slammed door startled both of us, and I jolted up. My mind started racing with all sorts of different thoughts about who it was, what their reaction was going to be, and how I could explain that me being on my parents' bed, clearly making out with another girl, was just . . . a joke?

I realized it was my dad, since he was going to take me to the airport, but after hearing the door slam, I didn't hear anything else from him. Thousands of ideas swirled inside my mind as I got out of bed and placed my hand on the doorknob, bracing myself for whatever retribution was awaiting me on the other side. I opened the door, but no one was there. I stepped out with caution, as though the floor were on fire, and confirmed no one was there. Was it a ghost? A figment of my imagination? Did my conscience make this up as a way of telling me I shouldn't have done what I did?

The only indication that there was anyone there was the fact that all the boxes I'd packed for the trip were missing. At first I thought I misplaced them, but no, they were all gone. That alone was confirmation that my dad was here and had taken all of my things somewhere.

Thankfully, he didn't throw everything out on the lawn and leave; most likely he'd gone to the airport ahead of us and was waiting there.

After I caught Jade up on the situation, she agreed to drive me to the airport, and she could see the anxiety written all over my face. Now my dad's retribution was an entire airport's ride away, and there was nothing I could do but watch the road go by and come up with some elaborate way of explaining myself. She tried her best to calm me down, but there isn't much anyone can do in this type of situation.

Finally, after what felt like hours, we came up to the airport terminal where my flight was taking off. But we didn't see my dad anywhere. As we pulled into the terminal, Jade pointed out, "Hey, isn't that your stuff right there?"

I squinted and my blood went cold. It was my luggage, but there was no Dad in sight. He'd done this on purpose. He'd dumped off all my things as a way of showing his disapproval. There wasn't any talking my way out of this one, especially without anyone there to talk to. All I could do was swallow my anxiety and apologize profusely to Jade as I hurried out of her car to catch my flight.

Jade apologized profusely for all that was happening, but I explained that it was my fault. I should've left her in the car back at my house, and this whole summer would've had a pretty bow on top of it. There was no turning back, though, and I held onto the bracelet as I made my way through the airport terminal.

Without any cellphones, all I could do was hold my breath throughout the entire plane ride to LA and try to come up with some excuse, some story I could weave that could get me out of this situation. Everything felt like it had been going well, like I was growing into the person I was meant to be, and now everything was set back. I was finally comfortable and found a woman I loved, and now that felt like a distant dream as I looked out at the clouds.

Now what? What am I supposed to do with my life now? How am I supposed to live? How am I supposed to survive this?

In the span of maybe twenty minutes, my whole life was flipped on its head, and for the first time in a long while, I felt truly alone.

Chapter 5

The Fallout

Judgment, Summer 1990

The hour-and-a-half plane ride to LA felt like an eternity. Each time I closed my eyes, I begged for the experience to have been just a dream. Every second I was in the sky, I was free. From thirty thousand feet in the air, there wasn't anyone who was going to judge me, no one who was going to question, scorn, or hate me. I dreaded every second that passed by, as each was another second until I faced judgment. I felt like I was on trial with the deliberations happening behind closed doors, and all I could do was await the jury's answer. I could only imagine what my parents were saying to each other, what they were telling my sister, who'd be picking me up at LAX.

I tried to think about what I could say in my defense. "No, Dad didn't catch me kissing a girl, she was just . . . telling me a secret and our lips got in the way." Poor excuses were the only things I could come up with. There was no explaining this one away.

With the airplane descending into LA, my anxiety level grew, and I dreaded every step I took in LAX. Maybe I could run away in a taxi? Sneak onto another plane and move to Canada and say I was a refugee from my parents? Not the most likely answers to my problems.

As I made my way through the busy airport traffic toward my bags, I tried to keep my cool. *Maybe my parents hadn't even said anything to my sister. Maybe they mistook the situation and were thinking that this whole thing never happened. Yeah, that's definitely a possibility*! Maybe I could just pretend like everything was normal. Like I was normal.

My sister spotted me in the pick-up lane, and I loaded my bags into her car. I got inside, trying to keep calm while she gave me a once-over like she was planning what to say. "So Dad told me what happened."

I swallowed hard. "Yeah? About what?" I tried my hardest to pretend like nothing had happened.

"He said you were not welcome back at the house after he caught you with that . . . girl."

The words washed over me like a cold bucket of water: "Not welcome back." I could feel her glaring at me as I tried not to make any sort of eye contact.

"Did that actually happen?" she asked.

A cold chill came down my spine. There were too many things to process in those few seconds and not enough time to come up with a good response, especially to your parents telling you they don't want you home anymore. All I could think about was whether my sister would even drive me back to her apartment if I told her the truth. The only thing I could think about was not being homeless over this, especially in a city I barely even knew.

"No, of course not," I said. "Dad was just mistaken and didn't see things right, y'know? He only saw a glance and possibly mistook what he thought he might've seen. That's it." I tried to declare it as though it were the truth.

There was a long pause before she responded with suspicion written all over her face, "Is that right?"

I tried to meet her eyes with some sort of conviction. "Yes. I swear."

Her eyes met the front of her car again. "Okay then." She put the car in drive, and we made our way back to her apartment.

It was a silent car trip with little more than quiet conversation made between us. There wasn't much more to say, and I wasn't eager to say much more than I already had. I was caught up in processing what my parents had said to my sister: "We don't want you back home." Those words were a stain on the front of my mind that I was desperate to clean. The only way I could think of was to just pretend like it didn't happen when I told my parents I made it to LA. And that's exactly what I did.

When we got back to my sister's apartment, I was worried our parents wouldn't even answer the phone. Mom picked up the line, and I could hear the defensiveness and hurt in her voice when I told her it was me. She at least sounded relieved that I'd made it safely.

"Is it true?" she asked. "Those things your father told me?" I could imagine how long she'd been mulling over what to say.

"No, Mom, I swear." I told her the same lie I told my sister.

There was a part of me that wanted to believe that lie myself, to pretend like the whole thing never happened, pretend like who was in that room wasn't me anymore. I think she wanted to believe that too. Both of my parents did.

There was a long pause before she spoke again. Relief but also distrust came through her voice. "Okay, because he thought he saw something more."

"No, Mom, trust me. Nothing like that happened." I told my dad the same thing shortly after and, from what I could tell from his voice, he believed me.

In a way, I started to believe it too. I tried in vain to convince myself that the lie was the truth so that all the questions and doubts about me would stop. Or maybe my dad was hoping he was wrong, that what he saw was a glimmer of light from the window obstructing his view. Before I left for LA, he only saw two gals being pals. After all, women are more intimate with each other as friends, and that's okay. The important thing in my parents' minds, in all my family's minds, was that they still had someone they could call their daughter and a sister. They accepted the lie with earnest and hoped the gay me was dead and buried, both in their minds and in my heart.

Starting from Scratch, Fall 1990

The topic was never brought up again, much to my relief. My family wasn't keen on asking more questions about it, and I wasn't keen on sharing anything more about myself. It was to everyone's benefit, yet I still felt like an imposter as I continued to lie about my sexuality to my family but was still out to all my friends who cared about me. The guilt started to build, and it wouldn't go away until I finally came out many years later.

Within a day, I went from cultivating a pride in who I was to constantly worrying about whether I was doing enough to please my family. I felt like a fragile figurine trapped in a glass closet. I could feel and see all the pain I'd caused but couldn't escape the prison of being closeted. I was in despair for a change in my life, one that would give me peace and happiness to be my true authentic self.

"Here, this is the best I got for you," my sister said while showing me her couch, which would serve as my bed. She lived in a tiny one-bedroom apartment in lovely Culver City with her boyfriend. It was home to the illustrious *Wheel of Fortune* film studio and away from the comfort of Malibu living I envisioned when I visited her to celebrate her graduation, but hey, it was better than going home to disapproving parents.

"Let's see how we can make it work, and remember, it's only temporary. This place is tiny enough as it is." I nodded, accepting the terms of living with her. I didn't want to rock the boat, and I tried to minimize myself as much as possible, especially since there were three people now living in this box, similar to what I imagined the boy in the bubble experienced.

Much like when we were growing up, we didn't really get along, yet we tried the best we could. It was similar to living with a roommate only because it makes the rent cheaper, except she was nice enough not to charge me. Interactions with each other were minimal, and the close quarters didn't make things better, but I was just grateful to have a place to stay.

After the incident, Jade and I sent each other letters back and forth, asking how each was doing. I gave her my new address to keep in touch while we were apart, and I diligently collected any mail sent to my sister's house, hoping she wouldn't catch on and tell my parents about my secret love notes.

Jade apologized for what happened and felt just as guilty as I did about it. I told her it was my fault, that if I'd just gotten out of the car none of this would've happened. It was comforting to at least have someone I could "talk" to about the real me. Unfortunately, it was a comfort that didn't last. Her initial concern after we were caught didn't turn into overwhelming support a few months down the road. We'd send each other pictures with our letters and tell each other how we were doing and what was happening in our lives. I told her I was taking night classes at a junior college and planning to apply to a prestigious college in Southern California, and she told me her plans of going to the University of Nebraska and her hopes for the future. But after a few weeks of conversations about our plans for the future, things slowed down. I sent Tracy Chapman lyrics professing my love, and she sent me some sentimental words back, but eventually her responses could be summed up today as one-word texts.

It was disheartening, and I could see the writing on the wall even if I didn't want to believe it. I wanted to hold onto something, something that was fully me, but eventually the letters stopped coming. I'd check the mailbox at the usual time only to find nothing. I thought, *Maybe she's just late writing one, so I'll check again tomorrow . . . Okay, nothing yet, but maybe the mailman mixed it up with something else and it's just late?* A few days passed and nothing still. *Maybe the entire postal system collapsed and it'll just be super late, right?* After a few more days, I took the hint that she wouldn't be writing any more letters and had moved on.

After that whirlwind summer, Jade and I never spoke again. It was again time for me to step back into the real world. Aside from Kim, I knew next to no one in this city, and I had to always keep up the appearance of being straight. I couldn't disappoint her or my parents again.

The darkness of the closet surrounded me, and it felt like the only refuge was making my parents proud of me, doing the best I could to try to be someone they could be proud of. I fed into the lie and tried to be a proud straight woman, no matter the cost.

Straight Pride, Spring 1991

By my second year of college, and with the fallout from my family drama, I was no clearer about my future than when I was sitting in Mrs. Bond's office only a few years earlier. I continued taking classes and focusing on a psych degree, but a keen interest in politics led me to change my major midyear, to political science. I'd always had an interest in politics, and I realized that I wasn't really enjoying the art of psychology as I thought I would. School had come very easy for my siblings, but I was always, and still am, the white sheep of my family when it came to academia. Although later in life, I was the first to earn a master's degree, I still had to work ten times harder to earn it.

In a roundabout way, being a political science major was exactly what I needed. I met Jackson in Economy 102. He sat right behind me, so I never got a good look at him, but I knew he had a bit of a crush on me. When I met him, I wasn't sure whether I was the straight woman of his dreams, but I certainly thought I could be. He was adorable and had the deepest, most piercing blue eyes I'd ever seen. He was a bit overweight, but I didn't care because he was funny and had the biggest heart. I did and still adore him to this day. Knowing next to no one in LA aside from my sister, I tried my best to make friends with everyone in my classes, and thus began my adventures with Jackson. It was exactly what I needed to stay sane, at least for a while.

I didn't know how deep in the closet I'd go once my relationship with him began. I learned how to shut out my feelings and urges to be loved by another woman, and I dove into this new love. From the moment we were introduced, we hit it off, and this progressed after our first dinner date. We jumped in headfirst, and suddenly

I had a boyfriend I was attracted to and truly enjoyed spending time with. We were inseparable. You could pluck our relationship from any cheesy romance movie. Everything was picturesque. He was supportive, caring, and giving.

It seemed as though I could live in the closet forever. On top of that, both his parents and mine were pleased with our relationship, and I found I could be open with my mom about Jackson in a way I never could with a woman. I learned how to be a proud straight woman, and I really played the part well.

The difference between my relationship with Jackson and the ones in those romance movies is that Jackson and I never had much in common. We came from two different worlds. He was a cisgender White guy who came from new money and still lived with his parents in a big house in Hancock Park. He even belonged to the same golf country club in Brentwood where OJ Simpson infamously played. As a closeted Black woman from the biggest little city in the world, I made every attempt to fit into this new world. Jackson believed I deserved to be brought into his world, and he showed me off without a care in the world. It was wonderful, yet I was in limbo given I felt I was living a lie. Ironically, I fit in seamlessly in this new life, which surprised me as well.

Both of my parents wanted their kids to have better lives, and they knew part of that was teaching us how to treat everyone equally regardless of class status. My status aside, Jackson's family loved me when he introduced me to them a few months later, and soon after he taught me how to play golf. It became a hobby I still enjoy today, albeit with minimal success improving my handicap. Then again, we can't all be Tiger Woods.

His parents weren't the only ones happy with their child's dating choices. Upon my parents hearing I was finally in a relationship with a nice man, I could hear the roar of excitement all the way from Reno. And not just because he was a great guy who treated everything and anything around him with the most respect, but also because I was dating a man.

"He sounds wonderful! I can't wait until I see where this goes!" and "He just better be good to you. I want you to be happy regardless of his race" were comments that became constant for the next couple of years while Jackson and I dated. Although my parents never met him, I knew that my regular calls to them during which I'd describe our excursions, as well as my sending photos home, were sources of comfort to them that I was not going astray.

Every day spent with Jackson was filled with activity after activity. We spent a week at Catalina Island, and there were many family events, including weddings, funerals, holiday parties, and concerts. The list was endless. It was as if I were filling the time to avoid the inevitable feeling that something was missing, and that struggle made it impossible for me to feel like I was doing the right thing. Even though there was mutual deep love and respect throughout our four-year relationship and we shared a handful of romantic interludes, it made me sad for him because I felt I was robbing him of the opportunity to be loved deeply. When we did make love, especially the first time, all I could do was stare blankly up at the ceiling, wondering when things would end. As much as I loved and adored Jackson, I was still contemplating my existence and questioning how I even got into this situation. Why couldn't I just enjoy it like every straight person on the planet? It's sex, not rocket science. What was wrong with me?

Despite all this, Jackson was always patient and only ever did things the two of us wanted to do, with the exception of one day while golfing. I was turned off by the way I was stared at when he and

I entered a room at the club. I could feel the looks of disappointment, or least perceived disappointment, and I remarked to him, "Why is everyone such an asshole here?"

He calmly replied, "Maybe *you* are the asshole."

I was shocked, but he was right. Why wasn't I giving these people a chance? Maybe it was because there were absolutely zero people of color or anyone who felt real to me (not counting OJ Simpson; he'd left a long time ago, and this was before the sad events of June 1994).

Jackson was always supportive and never pushed, but he did have a mind of his own and didn't hold back when his belief systems were questioned. It was also the first time I'd ever dated a Republican. I never thought about it, but I recognized that he and I were on different sides politically. Still, I knew how to acquiesce, as many of my close and dear friends were Republicans. I loved Jackson, but that didn't mean I had to agree with him. It was also the first time I was experiencing straight love, and I hoped that dating someone as great as him would make me straight, or at least unbend the arrow a bit. Everything would be great then.

But my parents were happy, especially my mom, who was impressed by Jackson's family history and fortune. I never once thought about the importance of money in this relationship, and even if we were to have married, it was his family's money and status, not mine. I sought love and understanding.

I knew I could make my own way and didn't need Jackson to do that. I just needed to be happy with myself for once.

The Party Apartment, Summer 1992

Part of adapting to a new relationship and city was the need to meet new people. I wanted to spend as little time on my sister's Malibu

Barbie couch as possible and instead meet new people. My new college setting was the perfect way to do that, and along the way I met two sisters who completely turned my world upside down, Isabelle and Felicia.

I met Isabelle through one of our classes, and we became friends during our semester together. When I mentioned to her that I was living out of my sister's one-bedroom apartment, she was horrified. She told me she and her sister, Felicia, were looking for a roommate so they could move out of their mother's basement, and she asked if I'd be interested.

In my mind, anything was better than living on a couch, so I took their offer without thinking. The next thing I knew, I was living in a pitch-black basement with no windows and barely any light, nicknamed "The Dungeon." Maybe not my best move. Still, it was better to be in an apartment where I could talk with the people I was living with, even if I was living in what felt like a black hole and missed a number of classes because of it.

Luckily for me, The Dungeon wasn't my resting place for long. Soon after, my mom received a large inheritance from an uncle who passed away, and she graciously agreed to help me get into a proper two-bed, two-bath apartment. My idea to the sisters was that since we were already living together, they could move in with me and we could all split the rent and other expenses.

From the outset, everything looked great. I'd finally have a place I could set up and call my own, and I had two people who'd be chipping in to help with rent. Much like a lot of other college experiences, however, things rarely turn out the way you expect them to.

The next couple of years were inundated with parties and lots and lots of liquor. I let myself go inside that apartment, and the sisters were always happy to take me along to whatever party they were going to next.

We went to all sorts of parties where everyone was celebrating whatever was happening. I've never been to as many dances, weddings, and backyard get-togethers in such a short amount of time as I did then. I was twenty-two years old, free, and ready to party whenever the mood struck. I vaguely remember going to a party that lasted until 6:00 a.m. Apparently my stamina knew no bounds. Oh how things have changed, as my regular bedtime today is no later than 8:30 p.m.!

What started out as a quiet studious home ended up as a party apartment, where the only things happening were someone drinking or recovering from drinking. Parties would last until dawn. It was during this time that I learned how to drink like a proper college student. It was also when I developed my love for the best drink on the planet, and amaretto sour. It's my drink of choice to this day. One night of debauchery, one of our frequent flier partiers spent the night and woke up still drunk the next day. She asked with a straight yet unsober face, "Do we have any more alcohol to drink?" After we all said in unison, "No, you drank everything we had," she promptly went into the bathroom to find the rubbing alcohol. Thankfully she was joking, but I think if we hadn't stopped her, she might've actually tried it.

That's what I lived with for years, and for a while I indulged. I drank to the point of having someone hold my hair above my face while I puked, then do it all again the next month, week, or day. I just wanted to live in the moment, to put everything about my identity behind me and let it fade as the alcohol took over. And for a while, it felt good not worrying about anything, just going with what everyone in the room wanted, being a part of something even if I knew next to no one there. Even when it was celebrating the wedding of someone I didn't know, I showed up ready to party.

As most stories about drinking and not having the best mental health go, I made some terrible decisions while drunk. I poured my feelings into the bottom of empty liquor bottles, and in those moments I had periods of drunken wanting, to be desired and to let go of any expectations people had placed on me. In those moments, if I needed something I got it.

One night after finishing a bottle, I was with Isabelle alone in a room. I don't remember what we were talking about, but something brought us together. Maybe it was me, maybe it was both of us feeling a need to be wanted. Regardless, we had sex. In the moment it felt like what I needed, like what I'd been hiding for years was finally coming out of me again. The real me, not some lie I was telling everyone around me. Having sex with her for the first time, I felt like I could be me.

After it happened, however, I felt disgusted. Waking up the next morning, I felt sick to my stomach from the night before . . . and then I rolled over to see who was in bed with me. Much like those cheesy rom-coms in which two people wake up next to each other not remembering what happened the night before until they realize who's in bed with them, I didn't want to believe it. I didn't want to accept what I'd done. Not only had I cheated on Jackson, but I wasn't supposed to be gay. I wasn't supposed to be doing this.

Isabelle woke up soon after, as if nothing ever happened. She looked at me puzzled, trying to figure out why I looked like the definition of an existential crisis. "It's not that big of a deal, Kelli," she assured me. "We just keep this between us and pretend like nothing ever happened."

Pretend like nothing ever happened? Yeah, of course. This was just a one-time mistake. We had a little bit too much to drink, and the alcohol took over. It happens all the time, and I definitely won't make that mistake ever again. Nope. Never again.

Each time I hung out with Jackson and Isabelle, my mind raced with guilt over what I'd done. I kept a smile and pretended like everything was fine while my stomach felt like a tidal wave. Every day, I thought that this time would be the last and I could keep this lie going. It was a cycle of constantly thinking that things were getting better and then falling so low again.

One night, I was feeling extremely low and depressed while watching *Friends* as a way to just bury the year away by watching pretend friends on TV, and I drank an entire bottle of wine. I sat there thinking to myself, *What am I doing? I'm not doing well in school.* Maybe it was the alcohol I was consuming every weekend or the fact that I'd been unfaithful to my boyfriend. My life felt out of control. I had two roommates who were constantly inviting people over and had some difficulty paying the bills with me. The people I called friends were around only when there was liquor. *What is here for me? What am I doing here?*

❧ ❧ ❧

On the dark day of April 5, 1994, a few weeks before my birthday, I spent the day watching the news announcing the death by suicide of Kurt Cobain. Being that he was the frontman of Nirvana, my favorite band of all time, I could only imagine the amount of shit he must have gone through, what his life must have been like. If someone like him, someone so talented and seemingly on top of the world, killed himself, if someone like him fell into such a dark place, then what the fuck was I doing with my life?

I fell into my own dark place. I was so ashamed of all I'd done. Jackson had his faults, too, and no one is perfect, but he was the one shining light in my life, and I was fucking lying to him every day. I thought about that first day when I arrived. *What am I trying to prove by being here? Why did I even come here? Was it for someone else or for me?* I thought about the person I'd become since coming to LA and thinking I'd get the chance to grow, to get the chance to be me in a city where virtually no one knew me. There alone, I stared at an empty spinning bottle on the wine-soaked carpet in my living room and thought, *This isn't who I want to be. And this isn't who I am meant to be.*

That night I made a decision. I couldn't be here anymore. If I stayed here, I'd more than likely end up doing the same thing Kurt Cobain did. I needed a restart, and I couldn't hide from the truth anymore. I knew what I needed, and I was determined to accept it without fear of hurting everyone around me. At the very least, I needed to stop lying to myself.

The Lie Is Only as Convincing as the Truth, Winter 1995

For years I'd been telling myself that I could live the way my parents wanted me to. It felt like I had no choice: Be straight or lose your family. I already had my dad's nonverbal confirmation of how he felt when he dumped my luggage at the side of the airport terminal. I believed for so long that my life would be that discarded luggage if I accepted myself. But you can lie to yourself for only so long before it eats away at your being. The more you try to bury something, the more your mind lingers on what you buried. And right then, I needed to climb out of the grave I'd dug myself.

I told the sisters what I was planning on doing, and since our lease was ending soon we made the decision to part ways. At this point I was done with them and, for the moment, with my life in LA. Whatever they did, I didn't care. I regretted meeting them and the path I followed during our friendship. And yet, in a way, through all the bullshit I went through, they were the reason I was able to accept myself again. I regret what happened, yes, but hitting rock bottom was the only thing that was going to make me realize some things can't be buried. No matter what I did or who I tried to be, my body refused to accept the lie I was building for everyone else, the lie that I could be with a man and be happy, that I could be "normal" in my parents' eyes like my siblings and would marry a guy and have twenty kids (ouch). That's not me, and I had to come to terms with it. Even if I had to hide it, the sisters helped me reemerge from the darkest part of the closet to see a sliver of light on the other side.

I knew living with my parents again would be rough, especially since I no longer had to pretend I was something I was not. I finally accepted my truth: I was a lesbian. Nothing would take that away from me now. I would never say it out loud or talk about it, but at least living with my parents meant I wouldn't be tempted to constantly drink.

The day I left for Reno, I knew I needed to let Jackson know why I was leaving. Rather than having an adult conversation with him, I wrote him a note from my yellow notepad (the equivalent of a sticky note). The only thing I could manage telling him was that I needed to move back home to focus on myself. I couldn't be in LA anymore, and it was killing me. I told him about the downward spiral my well-being had taken over the last month from partying every week, as well as what was happening and what I'd been feeling. Before going to the airport, I left it at his door.

Three days later I called him. I came out to him completely, and to my astonishment he was gracious. He said, "The most important thing is that you're happy and okay. That's all I want for you. No matter where you end up or where you go, know that I'll bc rooting for you."

It was a bittersweet moment. I was grateful to have his support but felt terrible for dumping him like this and running away. Even if it was what I needed, it still felt good to know that no matter what, he cared about me. And we've been friends ever since.

All in all, I'm glad for the relationship I experienced with Jackson. I learned that there are good men out there, men who know how to treat someone right. In my mind, he set the standard of what a boyfriend and a partner can look like in a relationship. He showed me what it was like to love someone unconditionally and be loved unconditionally in return. That relationship and now lasting friendship is something I hold close to my heart even now.

In leaving for LA, I was leaving for a better life. Or so I thought. I wanted to believe I was going to make a mark for myself, yet there I was going home with nothing to show for it. Well, almost nothing.

I left Reno shaken, wondering what was going to happen to me. I didn't know what to do or who I was going to be after being caught by my dad, and now all I could do was put one foot in front of the other. I didn't know where I wanted to go, but at least I knew who I wanted to be. I wanted to do things for me and no one else. And hey, maybe when I was ready to tell my parents the truth, they'd be ready to hear it and accept it. That's what I believed, and that's what I hoped for during my plane ride back.

Chapter 6

Trial by Fire

Welcome Home!

Stepping off the plane in Reno felt surreal. Instead of finding all my luggage dumped off at the side of the terminal, I was welcomed with open arms by my parents. They were ecstatic to have me back in their home again, and I was glad to live rent-free again.

In all seriousness, it was nice to see them so excited to have me back home, despite my not having much to show for being away. In their eyes, they were just happy to have one of their kids so close to them again, and for a time it was appreciated. They gave me the chance to have a reset, to try to figure out which direction I wanted to go. It was nice, but the reality was I just felt lost, like I was being sucked into quicksand and trying to find anything to grab on to, anything that would help me get out of the seemingly never-ending vacuum that was swallowing me whole.

Around the same time, my high school friends were graduating from college and celebrating their new degrees. I was happy for them and excited to see them as they came home to celebrate with their families, but it didn't help the sinking feeling within me. While my friends were plotting their next steps in their future careers, I was taking up odd jobs to get any sort of income, the worst of which was spending about nine hours a day picking up acorns from Lake Tahoe for a science experiment at a nearby university. The total amount for the extremely engaging and hard days of labor? About $50 per day. Not terrible, but I definitely don't recommend it as a career choice. For me, that was play money, money I could do whatever I wanted with. But if present-day Kelli were alive back then, she would've saved so much more of that. I didn't realize how much of an opportunity I had because I was so focused on what was right in front of me.

Throughout my two-year stint in Reno, I experienced loneliness and disinterest in life. For years I tried to disassociate myself from that abysmal time of my life. It was also a time of sadness followed by awakening. During the first few months of my return, my aunt Betty passed away, sending us all, especially my mom, into a spiral of grief for many reasons. For me it was the loss of an aunt who'd experienced trauma, mental illness, and chronic disease. As devastating as her death was, I felt a sense of relief that she was no longer in pain and despair. For my mom, it hit her extremely hard because Betty had been a true friend and confidant to her since their adolescence, and saying goodbye proved to be a difficult, heartbreaking journey. Our family was resilient, but Betty's death was one that haunted us for years as the joy and light within my mom inexplicably dimmed for months afterward.

Unfortunately I continued down my own spiral of despair. I was working graveyard shifts delivering blood to hospitals, yet another odd job I'd taken up to keep myself busy. The shifts were brutal (10:00 p.m.–7:00 a.m.), and I was often daydreaming and loopy at the end of them. One of those loopy days, I got into my dad's old '79 Buick, which he'd given me to use for work. What I didn't realize at the time was that this old rust bucket had some issues with the brakes. So after I turned on the car's ignition to warm it up in the cold of morning, I left it running and went back inside my work building to pick something up.

As I headed back outside to where my car was, it was mysteriously gone. I started to panic and thought, *What the hell happened to the car?! No one would want to steal this old rust bucket, so where is it?* I'd left it parked on a hill, and as I turned my gaze toward the bottom of said hill, I noticed the remains of two cars that had collided. Well, it was more like two cars were connected like puzzle pieces. As I put two and two together, the blood drained from my face. At least it hadn't been stolen, but now I was left with this.

What occurred remains the most unusual collision possible. While the car was running, the brake slipped and it rolled down the hill, striking the car in front and resting on the other car. There was no person behind the wheel when the accident occurred, which made it a phantom car crash. Present-day me would've done something completely different from what Kelli of the 1990s did. Today I would call the police and report what happened, but in my mind at the time all I could think was, *Oh no! I need to get the hell out of here!* So I went to my car and assessed the damage, which surprisingly wasn't much, then decided the best course of action was to just leave and hope no one noticed—though the loud screech of metal ripping against metal as I removed my car from the other didn't make me feel any better about what I was doing.

When I got home I immediately fell asleep, hoping to put the whole matter behind me. Next thing I knew, I was awakened by my dad telling me the police were at the door and asking for me, charging me with a hit-and-run and reckless abandonment. Both the police and my dad demanded an explanation for what had happened. As I pleaded my case, my dad used his experience as a former officer to talk them out of arresting me. Luckily they didn't, but they did cite me and told me I was going to be needed in court, a realization I saved for after I got some sleep.

On the day of my court date, I was freaking out. I pleaded my case to the judge in a panicked state as though I were a child trying to explain to her parents why she hadn't cleaned her room before they got home like they asked her to. I was rambling and trying to make this insane situation sound like it made sense. After I finished pleading my case, the judge called for a recess and asked to see me in his chambers. In my mind, I thought, *This is it. I'm going to be arrested, thrown in jail, and fined god knows how much, and there isn't anything I can do about it.*

I meekly went inside the judge's chambers, where he said to me, "You have a highly unusual case that doesn't warrant the citation you received."

As I looked into his eyes, I pictured myself going to the big house and starting the first lesbian chain-gang.

"However, you did leave the scene of a crime, and for that I'm going to charge you for bail."

Even though I was never arrested and it never affected my driving record, I took any sort of mercy I could get. The judge charged me $165 for a hit-and-run, and when I happily handed him my credit card he quipped, "You can hold onto that, as that's not part of my job here."

The entire experience felt like a blessing more than luck. I was blessed to learn the lesson that the truth will literally set you free.

I was blessed there hadn't been anyone in the other car when mine collided into it and that something worse hadn't happened to me. And I was blessed that this was resolved with what felt like the equivalent of getting my car towed.

On the outside things resolved themselves and I had everything working in my favor, but I still felt a sinking feeling. Every day was a struggle, and every day I felt like I was still walking in the dark, trying to find the light switch. I was no closer to finding that switch here than when I was living in LA.

After about a year and a half of living back home, I found a small gleam of light in the form of an invite to Steven's graduation party in Washington State. He had just graduated from a unique state college in Olympia and invited friends from across the country to come celebrate with him. I took the first flight out, as this was one event I was not going to miss.

Being in Washington was the breath of fresh air I needed. Not just because Washington is known for its intense rain that produces lush greenery, misty mountains, and coffee culture, but also because I love the culture and the diversity of people. I appreciated the carefree lifestyle and softness of the Washingtonians I met that weekend. Whatever it was, it felt idyllic, and I soaked up every second I could while I was there.

It was great to catch up and see Steven years after the party house in Reno. We gave each other the CliffsNotes versions of how our lives had been, but I didn't want to take away from the room, or the partying, by getting into the roller coaster of drama my life had been for the past few years. So that night, the whole group of friends Steven invited went all out with music, dancing, and socializing. You name it, we did it. I think everyone in that room needed that night out to just have fun. We had a lot to celebrate.

The next morning, my body was immediately filled with regret, but my heart felt full for the first time in a while. I felt like I had somewhere I belonged again, and I could just be me for once without having to constantly look over my shoulder. But then all the memories from the night came flooding back. I remembered people dancing, Steven and his friend doing a killer duet of Soft Cell's "Tainted Love," and making out with one of Steven's friends, Ashley.

After we all awoke we decided to go out for brunch. With all of us barely conscious from the night before, we stumbled in shambles into a local diner, where we got to catch up and get to know each other. Ashley was a close friend to Steven and had just broken up with her partner. Something about her drew the two of us close together. She certainly wasn't my type initially, as I'd never been with a woman of color, but she was nice and we enjoyed our night together. She also had a secret: She had a boyfriend she still loved who lived in another state.

Looking back I don't know what it was that brought us together. Maybe we were just two lost souls trying to make some sense of the world. Regardless, we hit it off extremely well, and she invited me back to Seattle to come visit her sometime. My immediate reaction was, "Absolutely yes!" A nice girl I'd already hit it off with was inviting me to come stay with her for a bit in a new city I was starting to love. How could I say no? So after a couple of months of saving up some money, I was back in Washington.

The second time only cemented what I felt the first time I visited. I loved Seattle, and I envisioned myself living there full time. With its lush green landscape, beautiful tall buildings, and gay district, it was the heartland of openness, and I couldn't wait to explore it more. Ashley gave me the full tour of the city, and every time I said something like "This place is incredible," she tried to encourage me to make it real: "You should come out here! Steven's here, and I'm here too!"

It was nice to think about, but the more I did, the more questions I had about how I'd make it work. There were not only logistics questions about how I'd move up there but also concerns about money and what I'd be able to find for work with only a high school diploma.

Returning home to Reno was exhausting and predictable. I felt lost and unsure of my next steps, and I could not get the thought of moving to Seattle out of my mind. What did I have here in Reno? What was I going to do here with my life that I couldn't do in a place I actually enjoyed being in? Sure, rent was free, but there had to be something more than just working night shifts delivering blood to hospitals. The more I considered it, the more I thought, *What more do I have to lose?* At least being in Seattle I could be more open. Sure, life had been a bit of a struggle the past twenty-seven years, but I'd make it work somehow. Hell, I'd made it work for the past five years, and now I needed a fresh start to try to get something in my life going. And hey, a fresh start in a new city I'd visited only a few times before moving there, what could go wrong?

I called Ashely to ask her about the accommodations at her place. I needed a place to crash while I figured out what I was going to do and where I was going to live. She enthusiastically said I could live with her and her roommates, a married professional couple who agreed as well. That was all I needed to hear.

It took a few months, but I packed one suitcase and booked the next available flight to Seattle.

Let's Try This Again, Fall 1997

Tons of concerns still lingered in the back of my mind. Throwing caution to the wind feels great in the initial moment, but then you start to consider everything else about the decision that will drastically affect your life, and you start to feel that looming worry. I tried to keep those thoughts out of my mind as I got to the airport. *I don't know what will happen, but I'll figure it out*, I told myself. Oh boy, was I unprepared for the path my life would take over the next couple of years.

When I arrived at the airport in Seattle, Ashley couldn't pick me up for some reason, so I was on my own navigating the city and making my way to her house. Having been in the city only twice, I promptly told the taxi driver I had no idea where I was going. Ashely gave me the address, but I couldn't find where I'd put it, and I knew only the general location of her house. So for the next three hours (thank you, taxi driver, for your patience), we drove around on a hopeless quest to find it. *Definitely off to a great start*, I thought.

When I got to Ashley's, I called to tell my parents about my decision to stay. As far as they knew, this was just a trip up there to see friends and I'd be back soon.

"Hey Mom," I started. "So I need to tell you . . . I found my way to Seattle and I'm not sure if I plan to return home."

"What?! What do you mean you're not coming home?!"

"Well, I think I'm going to be staying here for a while, and I want to see what I can make of myself in this city."

"Kelli, I am shocked. You will have a home to return to, but are you sure about this? You want to just up and leave with nothing?!"

"It's what I need to do, Mom. I know something is pulling me out here, and I need to find out what it is."

"Okay . . . I will pray for you, as you will need God now more than ever. I love you," she said, then promptly ended the call.

I felt a cold chill. Was I doing the right thing?

Over the next couple of months, my situation didn't look that different from when I was in Reno, only now I was sharing a bed with a woman I barely knew and a house with two other roommates. After a few weeks together, Ashley and I began to grow closer and I started to relax a bit. But I still needed a job.

I continued to take up odd jobs to make ends meet, and money was always a struggle between the two of us. I was now living on my own and had to pay rent. The best I did was working at an appointment center making $7 an hour, with commission on each solid appointment. Companies used the call center to promote different products they were selling, and if someone received a coupon for some future service, they could call for help scheduling whatever service it was for. Over time, selling was something I got surprisingly good at, and I was on the fast track to management.

Things were going great by the time I got a call from someone who'd received a gift certificate for a free photo session for their newborn. No big deal; I got the appointment scheduled relatively quickly and thought nothing of it. When I got these calls, I had a spiel to new moms about what they needed to have ready for the photographer: a favorite blanket, toys, and most importantly the newborn.

A few weeks later, I received an incoming call from one of the photographers, who said he had a funny story to share about the last appointment I'd booked for him. I asked what happened, and he told me that he went to the appointment expecting a new mother with her newborn, but instead what he walked into was a room with a favorite blanket, a toy, and no newborn. When he saw a sex toy gently placed on the blanket, he asked, "Where's the baby?"

The client replied, "Baby? There is no baby; I am the baby." The photographer promptly and politely excused himself and bolted to his car.

That was the most interesting part of the job. But a job setting appointments, as exciting as it sounds, doesn't contribute much toward rent, and I needed to get another job in order to have some sort of fiscal stability. Seattle is also a city filled with activism; people there take to the streets to protest everything, from the World Trade Embargo to fighting for soft toilet paper in local restaurants. Okay, the latter isn't true, but you get the point. I felt it was my duty as a new Washingtonian to take up a grassroots activism job. It didn't pay great, and I worked tirelessly putting in long hours, but it gave me my first inkling of where my life would be headed decades later.

On my days off from the appointment center, I found work with Greenpeace, and our tasks were to go door to door to ask people whether they were familiar with our work for the environment and how they could help protect it. In those early days of climate-change reckoning, people didn't own smart cars, and phones were just plain not smart, so my spiel was lost on them and many doors were slammed in my face. As an introvert, I often relied on my "door buddy," as they were called, to give the entire pitch while I stood with a clipboard. I was constantly met with disinterested people who just didn't want to be bothered about something they felt was out of their control.

Ironically enough, I was surrounded by freshly graduated college kids with a burning desire to make a difference in the world. I was getting schooled by them about how to get that first foot in the door and into deeper conversations that would more often than not prompt people to take some sort of action with us. It wasn't easy, and it definitely felt like a bruise to any sort of ego I had at the time, but in the long run it was worth it. The twelve-year-old dreamer in me who wanted to be a lawyer and politically active in the world was still alive, and even though I was a starving activist, at least I was getting into something that involved politics and made me feel like I was making a difference. Even if it was only to a few people's lives, it still felt meaningful.

For about a year that was the routine of my life, constantly working and constantly worried about life's due dates. It became my routine, but over time Ashely and I grew closer over those constant routines. We were both committed to the idea of "figuring it out as we go," always holding out hope that something would happen and something would go our way whenever we had a crisis. And it usually did. Things were going steady, and then something changed.

We had found a nice little one-bed, one-bath apartment not far from our jobs. It had a classic look that appealed to us both, even an antique clawfoot tub that resembled one we used at an Airbnb we frequented in Olympia. To my knowledge, we were happy. Ashley's friend had just graduated from Evergreen State College and invited a few people over for a graduation party, including both of us. Naturally we went, and we had a good time doing typical college party stuff, but toward the middle of the night I wound up sitting on top of a hill and thinking about where my life was going. My thoughts were interrupted when I saw Ashley and her ex-boyfriend—the person she had broken up with right before she asked me to visit Seattle for the first time—talking intimately on the side of the house. I had no reason to think anything of it, but the image of the two of them stayed with me for the remainder of the evening.

Eventually I rejoined everyone in the main room, and for the rest of the night she and I never spoke of the interaction. It wasn't until the next day that I learned what actually happened between them.

"Um, there's . . . um . . . something I need to tell you," Ashley started.

I didn't have time to ask her what was up before she blurted it out.

"So me and Phillip . . . we saw one another a few weeks ago, and one thing led to another, and we slept together."

I didn't know what to say. The shock was palpable as blood quickly rushed to my head. It was a bag of mixed feelings. I thought things had been going steady between the two of us, but looking back I can tell we were already on the outs of our relationship. My feelings for her dwindled over time, and this only exacerbated those feelings.

"And it wasn't the first time."

Okay, now the bag of mixed feelings was an entire fucking ocean. "What do you mean, 'it wasn't the first time'?"

"Well . . . so before you moved here, I realized I still had feelings for him."

Again I was stunned. I didn't know what to say, how to react, how to feel, how to even begin processing the emotions welling up inside me. "Why didn't you tell me?!" I exclaimed. "After all this time we've spent together trying to get to this point in this relationship? We've gone through so much, and you're just telling me *now* that you still have feelings for Phillip?" I was shocked and just could not believe the words coming from her mouth. Or maybe I just didn't want to accept the purely honest yet painful realization that I needed to end this now before it went too far. Ashley was very clear about her feelings for her ex, those feelings were real, and nothing was going to change that.

For some reason that goes beyond my thinking today, I decided to stick it out and try to make it work somehow. Maybe it was because I didn't want to completely let go of what I was holding onto. I'd moved out there with no life plan and absolutely nothing besides a suitcase full of clothes, and here I still was with no real life plan.

And the person I was living with, the person I considered my girlfriend, had cheated on me. I needed to at least hold onto something.

Ashley apologized profusely to me, but I was torn about what I needed and really wanted to do going forward. I wasn't ready to forgo the little bit I had, but now I knew things were in serious decline, and I needed a change decided to finally move out and thereafter I moved away and return to single life. It turned out to be the right direction to take.

At the dawn of the internet was MSN messaging, and it was a revolution to be able to message people from across the globe who I'd never had any way of contacting or getting to know before. That's how I came to know a woman based in Chicago who was in almost an identical reality to mine. We were both on the outs of our respective relationships, and we both knew what we needed to do but didn't know how to actually do it. So instead of facing our situations head-on, she invited me out to Chicago for a weekend, which I happily accepted.

She gave me a tour of the city, and it felt so refreshing to be able to be with someone I felt so compatible with. She was incredibly smart, politically active, and carried an invigorating energy with her wherever she went. Soon after we met, we were in her bathroom making love to Green Day's "Boulevard of Broken Dreams," a song that completely illustrates how I felt emotionally, physically, and sexually. It could not get any more emotionally complicated.

There was a huge part of me that wanted to keep the weekend going, to keep seeing her, but I knew things wouldn't work out. Between the situation with her partner and her practically living halfway across the US, I couldn't put myself through the same situation I'd put myself with Jamie. So one weekend away never became more than just that, but I never stopped thinking about her and what

I needed. I also came to find out that Ashley had again met with Phillip while I was away. It wasn't like it was out in the open, but there was enough plausible deniability on both our ends to pretend like we weren't doing what we were doing. This time we both were caught up in our respective feelings for others.

You'd think that's where either one of us would've stopped and called it quits on the relationship, but no. We tried to keep this level of peace between the two of us and imagine that everything was fine, when clearly it wasn't.

Mail-Order Confession, Summer 1999

Something else was also weighing on my mind and I knew at this point I couldn't keep dancing around the topic whenever my parents or other family members checked up to see how I was doing. Since coming to Seattle, I had tried to skirt around the topic whenever it came up, telling whatever lie my parents could hear from me. Now I felt like I couldn't hide it anymore, and I wouldn't hide my partner from my parents. I knew this day would have to come eventually.

I finally mustered up all the courage I had in me, and I did the unthinkable, what I thought would be impossible as a child, and I grabbed a pen. Hell no, I was not going to call them! I needed that extra barrier between us and between responses because I didn't know what would come next if I called. So I wrote a lengthy letter explaining that I was finally comfortable enough with myself to say I was a lesbian and had been all my life. The letter was poignant and cathartic for me, as it was the first time in my twenty-nine years on Earth that I was honest about who I truly was. I was a woman who loved another woman, and there was no reason to remain in the dark closet I'd created for myself.

A few weeks later, I received an envelope from my mom. My heart skipped a beat when I saw the return address on the front. All the time since sending my letter, I never expected them to say anything, so I was shocked that they sent something back. Acknowledging my letter was far beyond what I ever expected from them. This was it. I was either going to get a warm hug and acceptance, or I was about to read the last message I'd ever receive from them.

I took a deep breath and ripped open the envelope. Inside was an acknowledgement that they'd received it, didn't agree with it at all, and Mom was worried about me going to hell. I even got an entire biblical passage about the fires of damnation or whatever. But at the very least, it wasn't a complete "It's probably best if you do not come home again."

I hadn't known what to expect from them, but to me the important part was having this off my chest. It felt like finally removing a heavy backpack after a long day; that relief you get in your shoulders after having carried two tons worth of textbooks is bliss, and I'd just released over a decade's worth of textbooks off my shoulders.

What caught me off guard was when my mom called soon after to tell me that in a month's time, she and my aunt were planning a trip up to Vancouver, BC, to get away and invited me to go with them since it was practically next door. I told her that if I went with them, I was going to bring Patricia, a woman, I had recently begun seeing seriously since I wanted my family to meet her. She told me that would be fine, and much to my surprise I felt this could be the start of a reconciliation.

The day they came to visit arrived quickly, and upon seeing me for the first time in over two years, one of the first comments my mom made was that she was surprised I hadn't cut my hair and didn't "look like a dyke on a bike." Those were her words, which I will never forget. I took it on the chin, thinking the weekend would serve to help my mom come around and accept me more. When Patricia greeted her warmly, my mom's expression changed. Now that she was in front of a guest, she put on her best behavior when addressing either of us.

We made our way up to Vancouver and got out of the car to start exploring the city. The trip was good, as my mom and aunt welcomed Patricia without drama or fanfare. Overall, the whole weekend went off without too many hiccups. Out of the sheer understanding that this was real and not just a friendship like all the others, my mom was a bit annoyed when I told her Patricia and I were absolutely getting our own room. Other than that, it was a fun getaway weekend together, and I'm just glad that the Good Book didn't get thrown at me during our time together. I can guess that my mom was equally relieved we didn't throw pride flags at them.

Toward the end of the trip, things felt like they were in a great spot. We were all enjoying ourselves and the Vancouver sights. Then my mom pulled me aside and said, "Kelli, you know I will always love you."

I nodded my head, but I knew there was more to the end of that sentence.

"You can always come home when you need to, but"—there it was—"we just can't talk about your lifestyle choice."

I gave a half-hearted response: "Sure, Mom, I love you too."

It wasn't the enthusiastic response I was hoping for after spending a weekend together with my partner, but it was again definitely better than being told I could never return home or never call again. No, that . . . would come later.

Chapter 7

The Rain Brings Rainbows

My Perfect Storm, Fall 1999

Everywhere I looked and with everyone I talked to, the topic always came back to the start of a new millennium. Some people thought it would be the end of the world, and some couldn't wrap their heads around the panic. I was just struggling, bouncing around from job to job, trying to make ends meet. After all, the supposed end of the world didn't stop bills from being mailed to me every month.

I ended up working for an innovative startup company called Zydeco.com (named after the Zydeco music scene in New Orleans, compliments of a CEO from the South). Like most startups around the time, this one was unique in creating an online shopping experience that was suited for customers. At the start of my employment, I was hired to be an assistant to the assistant (putting together the office furniture and other mind-boggling work). After a few weeks spent showing my worth in research, I was promoted to research analyst, working directly with the CEO and chief marketing officer. I was flattered yet scared, just happy to have a job even if I didn't know one thing about online shopping. Case in point, one of my research ventures was to shop online with the now infamous eBay. During my research, I accidentally attempted a bid to purchase a $450,000 plane! Thankfully I caught the mistake before it was too late. I clearly still had a lot to learn about online shopping, and as time progressed, I became a pro shopper, if only for my job.

The CEO was constantly thinking up new ways to invest and personalize the shoppers' experience. The company was fortunate enough to have purchased an innovative server from IBM that would allow a potential customer to create their own shopping experience based on a few simple questions of interest and style. It saw itself as being on the cusp of a classier version of Amazon during the dot-com boom when Amazon was just an unknown online bookstore.

After the first few months of employment, I realized my days and nights would be consumed by making this company successful. My days consisted of listening to the CEO rant, albeit intelligently, about algorithms and C++ programs, things that were foreign not only to me but probably even to him (I kid, he was a programmer by trade). By nightfall we were engrossed in programming and outlining the customer experience. It was invigorating, but I felt more exhausted than I'd ever felt in a job before. Was it worth the $40,000 salary I was making in 1999? It would prove to one of the most rewarding and disappointing times of my life, yet it prepared me for more exhausting work to come.

I was learning the ins and outs of marketing and branding, soon on my way to becoming one of the strongest partners to the CEO in that I was solely responsible for developing the psychological profiling questions customers would respond to when creating their shopping experience. One year after the company folded, it sold the algorithm and server to Amazon. I'm proud to say that I was part of history with my colleagues, who were really responsible for why you've been bombarded with questions about dishware all these years.

My work week suddenly shifted from fifty to seventy hours a week, and many days I wasn't sure when I'd be able to leave the cave to go home to the comfort of my bed. At the time, my home life was pretty shitty, and I was unhappy with my personal relationship. Thankfully, at the end of the year I was given a much-needed raise to $50,000 a year, which was more money than I could've imagined making at that point in my career. The CEO was constantly making promises such as, "We'll be the biggest company in town" and "You'll be able to retire at forty because our stock options will sustain you." Whatever. I was about to be thirty and was still unsure whether this was going to work out. If I were to believe what the CEO was telling the team, I would've thought he was Moses leading us to the Promised Land.

In hindsight, he was like many up-and-coming CEOs of the startup craze: hungry—hungry to get their ideas funded, branded, and operational. There are even stories of some who elected to end their lives over the loss of their businesses when the dot-com bubble burst in late 2001. Our fearless leader believed wholeheartedly that when we launched we'd all be making millions, and he'd do anything to make it happen. He filled us all with the promise that this was only a small price to pay and we'd all be able to afford our own private islands in the end.

At the time, everything was evolving at such a rapid pace and I was at the forefront, surrounded mostly by men, and I felt very powerful. I dare say, invincible. Even more so, I surprised myself with what I was able to do. I had never set a path for greatness and often felt limited by my lack of knowledge in the industry, but I realized that I did have the will to see this through and to do anything I could to make it real. For a while, it gave me a renewed sense of purpose. I never thought I could help build an algorithm, conduct marketing research, or help build something like this from the ground up. It was draining and exhausting for sure, but it helped me realize that the only limits I had to doing something were the limits I placed on myself. As much as I never considered myself to be one to follow the leader (a game I even hated when I was child), for some reason I was more than willing to follow the captain to whatever X he had on his map.

Days turned to weeks and weeks turned to months. Turns out building an algorithm that curates shopping experiences during the dawn of the internet isn't quick and easy, and it started to affect more than just company morale. Angel investors started to get antsy about their returns on investment, and on more than one occasion I witnessed our CEO becoming increasingly more stressed. "I can't pay them back until this thing moves," he'd often say, and I agreed. How can you disrupt greatness before greatness can take shape? The promise of millions still felt like a far-fetched idea, and people were starting to get anxious. For those of us in the trenches, we never lost hope. We invested blood, sweat, tears, and in some cases our relationships to see this venture through.

In an effort to increase team morale, our CEO asked a few of us in the inner circle to take a break. I didn't realize until we got to our meeting location that we were going to see the new George Clooney flick, *A Perfect Storm*. While I'm a huge Clooney fan, I didn't know much about this movie. Then I learned the premise was about a fisherman down on his luck who decides to head out late at night past his usual fishing area. Little does he know, a hurricane would take hold of the coast. While he does find success, he and his crew get caught up in the hurricane while trying to rush back to shore to salvage their haul. Things go from bad to worse, and the entire crew, along with their ship, gets swallowed by the storm. This was when I realized, *OMG we were the fools who couldn't get the fish or bring the boat back to shore. Fuck this, I want to get back to shore. I am not dying with these people!*

Why our CEO decided that "Hey you know what'll be a perfect thing to watch with the team? A movie about all its crew dying for a big haul" was a good idea I'll never know. Maybe he knew things were sinking, but he did not let that movie go under our radar. "We're all in this together! Just like in *Perfect Storm*!" he said, trying to help our morale (*trying* being the key word). Regardless, we kept with it. We were in too deep, and at this point everyone was going to see this through.

Thirty Is for Wimps, Spring 2001

Working at Zydeco felt like a never-ending well, and there was never a dull moment. One time our CEO decided he wanted to embed a chip into his arm that would allow his brain waves to be monitored. It became a joke for a while, until years later when this procedure became real. When I heard it had happened, I thought back to the days when I couldn't believe anyone in their right mind would want a chip in their arm or for a computer chip to monitor their every move, but welcome to Y2K.

The deeper I went into the well, the more I felt sucked in. I was also in love with making money at the time, and all I had on my mind were stock options and being as rich as my colleagues on the Eastside at Microsoft. I was too deep to see past my own hands, and I felt like I was falling. At the beginning, I thought, "We're going to be rich," but "I hope I make it out of here alive." My emotions were all over the place, and the uncertainty of it all was driving me crazy. As much as this job opened my eyes to the possibilities and opportunities I could create from nothing, the company was flatlining. The writing was on the wall, and I knew something needed to change.

I tried to spend what time I could in the office, focusing on the next thing that could help keep this company afloat, filling buckets and buckets of water and chucking it out of the ship as it continued to take on more. It was a desperate attempt to keep things going. Much like trying to do that for a real ship, it wasn't long before I might as well have been moving a bucket of water from one part of the ocean to a slightly different part. Meetings became less about what we could do to get things off the ground and more about what we could sell off to keep the lights on in the office.

Unfortunately, Zydeco was in the same boat as so many other dot-com startups: Everybody came into the industry thinking they were going to be the one that was different from the rest and become the go-to site for people to use. Many entrepreneurs became millionaires only to have the rug pulled out from under them. By 2000, the dot-com industry started to decline and funders were pulling out of investments, leaving Zydeco in the dust storm that led to the decision to close the business. It sold "Bertha," its trusted motherboard, to its archrivals at Amazon, and more importantly, I lost my livelihood. I felt certain I would still have some financial windfall from the sale, but Zydeco was told its stock was dead in the water.

Anger boiled inside me: "What the fuck was all this work for?! Now I'm left with nothing to show for it?" I felt completely and utterly alone in my feelings of loss, and nothing my partner did could console me. I was devastated. *What more can happen?* I kept asking myself time and time again. In 2001, my answer came like a ton of bricks being dropped on me.

I was turning thirty years old, and all around me were familiar faces of those hitting the same milestone. Old friends and colleagues were excited to share what their lives had been like and to start the next leg of their journeys. Some of them were starting to have kids, others had new careers lined up. The possibilities seemed endless for everyone else around me, and I was envious. Why did they get to have these seemingly perfect lives in front of them? From my perspective, they knew where they were going and what they wanted to do, and they were buying their dream homes and celebrating their three decades of being alive with champagne and presents galore. All I could do was grit my teeth and hold in all the resentment I felt as I joined in singing "Happy Birthday" from afar.

The day that I turned thirty, I didn't know what to expect, whether I'd get the same sort of treatment from family and friends. By this time, I'd found work at a nonprofit company as a coordinator, so on a dreary day in April, I went into the office. Coincidentally, my coworker Marcy shared the exact same birthday as me, and I walked in to find everyone focusing on the surprise party that awaited her. It felt like my lungs had been crushed. I couldn't bring myself to scream, and I certainly couldn't bring myself to remind them that we shared a birthday; no, that would spoil the moment.

A few minutes later I heard, "SURPRISE!" Everyone was excited and Marcy was especially gleeful, soaking in all the attention. I sat there in silence, taking everything in. Everything was loud, but my head felt quiet. All I could think about was why her? Why not me? Why did everyone around me get to revel in the joy of having people around them and not me? I could only watch as Marcy basked in everything I wished I had that day. She got the gifts, and all I got was a hollow feeling.

After coming home from work, I found no sort of celebration, not from Patricia nor my family. Nobody remembered and nobody seemed to give a shit. The world felt cold and empty. What was I doing with my life?

It's my belief that turning thirty is one of the most difficult phases in a woman's life. It's about turning a page and starting a new decade, a new chapter of life, and I didn't have anything to show for the previous three. The day I turned thirty was the first day I thought to myself, *I may be suffering from depression*.

It's easy to look back in hindsight with years of therapy and self-care behind me and see that I was more than depressed at the time and had been for a while. But at the time, turning thirty was like opening a deep cut that manifested into a wound that took me years to heal from. I knew something was wrong, and it terrified me.

At a young age, I learned from Aunt Betty about what it's like not to have the best mental state. It was quite uncommon in those days for families of color to speak openly about mental health, and my family was no different. It's one of those subjects we all know exists, but instead of addressing it we either ignore it outright or say things like, "Oh, that's just them" or "All you need to do is pray more." This was especially true with Betty. She was not only my mother's sister and best friend but was an extremely intelligent woman who was working toward her PhD in psychology before schizophrenia started to take a serious hold over her. She wanted to be a therapist and help those in need, and she was one of the first people in her family to graduate from college, the first to attend a PhD program. She was a proud woman who held a strong connection to her African roots and even gave my family an encyclopedia of Black history that we treasure even today. In my mind, she was revolutionary to our family, but I witnessed the gradual decline of her sanity every time I saw her.

Being that I was the youngest of my siblings, everything was kept from me. It was as if information funneled from my parents to my siblings and then stopped with me. When it came to Betty, this was certainly the case. There was always a tense atmosphere in my grandparents' house whenever we visited. Betty had purchased the home for them during the '70s, and she continued to live there with my other aunt, Shirley. The house had always been a safe haven for me between the ages of three and ten. But after I turned ten, I realized I never knew which Betty would greet me, whether it would be a nice, warm smile or a destructive outburst as soon as she laid eyes on me. She would shuffle through the house in a despondent type of way, as if she weren't aware of where she was. She was someone who needed help, but we didn't talk about it.

The caveat is that my mom truly loved Betty. She talked to, prayed for, and was there for her throughout every step of her illness. Though it was a three-hour trek to San Jose, we traveled there whenever we could to spend time with her and the family.

It was a lot to take in at an early age. There were so many stories that were told of Betty and how difficult life was for her, yet my grandparents were resolved to help her to the best of their abilities. I had yet to come to terms with what mental illness meant to me, especially in the '80s when it was the most taboo of topics. No one even named it schizophrenia until the late '70s or early '80s, when she finally allowed a psychiatrist to treat her. In my family, one of two things would help support Betty: prayer or medicine. Since Betty refused formal treatment, the family resorted to prayer. Although Betty never went to see a therapist or took anything to help, she was still mindful that something was hurting her mentally. It was like she was trapped in a steel cage with no access to the outside world. She wanted to try to resolve her mental illness on her own, but unfortunately, as time went on, things only got worse for her.

It reached its peak for me when my brother graduated from Stanford in the spring of 1983. We were all excited to see him graduate and had driven out to see him walk across the stage and accept his degree. It was supposed to be a proud moment we'd all carry with him. He was in good company, as evidenced by photos of him with the now-retired NFL quarterback John Elway. While we were at the ceremony, I was talking with my relatives when suddenly Betty came and grabbed my arm. Without any warning, she dragged me off somewhere; I don't remember specifically where, but I do remember being terrified. I didn't know what was going on or why I was being pulled away by Betty, but no one seemed to question it.

To this day, I still have no idea why it happened, but it showed how the illness had completely taken over her thoughts and life. As I grew older, I feared the same illness would take me, but thankfully I learned it doesn't work that way.

Betty continued to talk about foods that were harming us, and she often walked into the street naked. To everyone's anguish, no one knew how to help. It was as if the only way to address it was to act as if it were normal. Whenever the topic of seeking treatment for Betty came up, it became a touchy situation that no one wanted to formally address. We just didn't talk about her mental illness. But that moment left a serious impression on me.

Throughout the ceremony, I couldn't get what happened out of my head. When it ended, everyone gave congratulations to my brother and just moved on with their lives. I knew logically that there wasn't much I could do, but I still had deep empathy for Aunt Betty and what she was going through, and I wish I could've helped her through those times.

I told myself I'd seek help if I ever fell that far; if I couldn't help the person in front of me, I'd at least try to help myself and make sure I was able to stand on my own two feet. It was the same promise I made as a child with the hope I'd never have to resort to getting any sort of help. Now here I was, still feeling like I was in denial. Sure, I might be depressed, but I could still manage my life, right?

I tried to embody that stoic, proud sense of self my parents had instilled in me, and even as I started to realize something was wrong, I resisted seeking outside help. Even as things were crumbling around me, I wanted to keep the impression that everything was fine. Admitting things were going downhill fast meant reconsidering all my life choices up to this point, and nothing was preparing me to unpack what that meant.

Out of a Fire and Onto the Floor, Summer 2001

To cope with being emotionally despondent, I poured more hours and focus into my new job, which at least gave me the luxury of not having to focus on the root cause of my depression. At this point, it was already a routine. I tried to bury my feelings in something, anything I could find that was right in front of me, and I found myself falling victim to chat rooms. During the late 1990s and early 2000s, chat rooms were a craze. I could speak to anyone in the world, but it brought me empty joy. Little did I know it would also ruin me.

It wasn't because I was in love with another woman but because I was more in love with the idea of leaving my life in Seattle behind. I had sunk to the bottom of *The Abyss* and couldn't even signal to Ed Harris or Mary Elizabeth Mastrantonio for help getting me out safely.

Home Alone, Spring 2002

Day in and day out, my body was reaching its breaking point. Then there was a small glimmer of light at the end of the tunnel. Through pure chance, I found a listing for a small apartment to rent on the outskirts of Phoenix. It was a backhouse with no stove, but it had a futon, bathroom, and fridge. This was what I needed, and I wasn't going to let this moment fall through the cracks. I contacted the landlord and signed a leasing agreement almost immediately upon seeing the place.

Being on my own and starting to take hold of my own life gave me a sense of control I'd never felt before, at any point of my life. I was no longer living for someone or something else. I was starting to live for myself while trying not to hurt others in return.

Who would've thought that trying to find happiness in someone else was never going to work out or bring happiness to my own life? Certainly not me, and definitely not until I realized I needed to make myself happy and whole before I was going to make anyone feel the same. I needed to get help. I needed something to help balance my sanity and to make sure I didn't sink that low again.

Ironically enough, what I chose was to go back to church. Not a traditional church, because I wasn't about to put myself back in the flames of self-righteous declarations about how gay people don't fit in the world, but a gay church, a church where a rainbow doesn't trigger a three-hour-long rant about how gay people stole it from a leprechaun or some other mythical creature from folklore. I found a local metropolitan community church, one founded by and for the LGBTQ+ community. To this day I'm still a spiritual person, but I never felt safe at a traditional church, let alone in a community, and being in this queer-focused church felt like the second step I needed to take to move forward.

Being part of this new church experience was exactly what I needed. The community didn't care where I came from or what I did; they were just glad I was there. We were all brought together under one roof for the same thing. People accepted me and who I was without having to learn my backstory to know whether I was worthy of being in the room. For me it was the judgment-free place I needed to start making amends, not just with everyone I'd hurt but with myself.

It was also the place where I met a beautiful woman who reminded me of an angel sent from heaven. Her name was Dionne (named after the legendary singer of "Do You Know the Way to San Jose?"). I was attending my first real gay wedding when I saw her, and I was hooked as soon as she performed. She was a professional singer and often performed in metropolitan community churches around the country. During the song "the Lord's Prayer," she hit a high note that went into the stratosphere, and I instantly fell hard. She was a gorgeous woman of color, talented, and had all the confidence in the world. I was drawn to her and knew I needed to make a move, so I did so at the reception, introducing myself with a pick-up line for the ages: "Wow, you have a beautiful voice. I didn't know whether you were a professional singer or you had a gerbil up your ass."

She leaned into the joke and said, "I can see how you could be confused by that." I was smitten, and that was the start of a beautiful relationship. Years later she said it was the most endearing thing she'd ever heard. Thank god, because I'm not sure I could ever be that smooth or suave again.

Meeting Dionne felt like getting a second chance to be someone different in a relationship. We took things slow when we first started dating, taking the time to get to know each other before committing to anything. The two of us clicked from the first moment, and it felt like the best thing in the world to finally be with someone I felt compatible with in a relationship. We both had similar goals and ambitions in life, and she encouraged me to push myself to do things I never would've thought of.

With Dionne's support and encouragement, I returned to therapy. After confiding in her about what I'd been through and what I'd done, she made sure I had someone to talk to about anything and everything. It was through that work that I started to be honest with myself about what I was feeling and dealing with the depression that had built up over the years and was now taking a serious toll on anything and everything in my life. I longed for compatibility with someone I believed was truly worth my time, someone who loved me in all the ways I needed and wanted, and vice versa. Starting that journey wasn't easy. I had to be really honest with myself and come to terms with the consequences of my actions.

With each day that passed, I started to practice forgiveness, including toward myself for what I'd done and the people I'd hurt. I realized I was using relationships to soften my depression, trying to bury my feelings about my own failures in someone else, and that was never going to work. It served only to amplify and create traumatic moments for myself and those around me. In my relationship with Patricia, for instance, I was holding both of us emotionally hostage by not doing what needed to be done and by shirking away from being a responsible adult in the situation.

After so many years of trying and failing to find a direction for my life, I felt like I found it here, with Dionne. It was a feeling that there was finally a light at the end of a very dark and bumpy tunnel, and now I could start to heal. This was my fairy-tale ending where everyone lives happily ever after. At least that's what I believed for a while.

Me and Santa at age 3

Mom and Dad on their wedding day

Pigtails but Tomboy years, age 10

My beloved Grandparents with my parents outside the San Jose family home

8th Grade Prom with Manny and looking dapper

Senior HS PowderPuff Football with Angie and Jennifer.
I am happy because there were donuts

Maybe the first HS gay prom with Amy (not my date)

The Heterosexual years with Richard. Closeted yet smiling

Proud college graduate

Comedy days at The Comedy Spot in Scottsdale

First and only Houston Family selfie

Proudest moment accepting 2024 Puget Sound Business Journal Diversity Champion Award

Chapter 8

White Picket Fence

A New Vision, Spring 2003

Starting over from scratch isn't easy, and it never has an easy landing. Like accidentally jumping off a trampoline and landing on your ass, it's painful, it's hard, and your friends and family may think you're loony. But you get up again because you have to. No one but you is going to help you get back on the trampoline again, so that's what you do. And that's what I had to do. I started with practically nothing and worked harder than I ever thought I could to make sure I didn't land on my ass again.

Even before moving to Phoenix, I had aspirations to have something to strive for, but first I needed to start at the bottom. Ironically enough, I started taking online college courses that were long overdue, yet I was committed to doing it. I knew how important it was to have a degree, and with Dionne's support I started to seriously buckle down and take my studies more seriously. Taking up so many odd jobs because you don't have a degree wears on you.

During the first year of our relationship, I began work at a behavior health agency as a foster care specialist. I wasn't happy with this role and was always looking for something more. It was at this point I decided to go into consulting with a former foster care provider who owned a large number of group homes in the area. We made an agreement that I would help build her business with various tasks. She asked if I could be her liaison to the state of AZ and provide training to her staff. This was the type of opportunity I felt I needed to get my consulting business off the ground. She offered to pay me more than what I was making in my current position, and I jumped at the opportunity to leave that job and go into business for myself. Looking back, I must have been crazy to take this plunge, but I really thought I could do it.

With only one promising client, I created Vision Consulting, a Jill-of-all-trades consulting business that focused on training, business development, licensing, and more, was a dream for me because it was everything I wanted to do at that time. While I enjoyed being my own boss, it became a bit of a financial burden that fell all on me.

I was prepared for anything my client would throw my way, but I wasn't too keen on working inside the homes. For context, group homes at that time housed many children of various ages and backgrounds, most of whom had experienced unimaginable depths of trauma and abuse. At times it was scary to hear their stories. One such story was about a three-year-old girl who'd been molested by her father and was taken from the home, and other stories detailed children who were the abusers. It took a superwoman like my client to take on these homes and provide more stability. The darker side of abuse, neglect, and trauma is that many children within this type of group home often show aggression without any fault of their own and are often heavily medicated. It's sad and disheartening, but the reality was that my client's team were experiencing these aggressions and in need of training to address them.

My next task as her consultant was to train over one hundred staff members in restraint tactics. As a certified trainer, it taught me a lot about people and compassion. This work shouldn't be about restraining or holding a child down (which is illegal, by the way) but about teaching a child compassion and communication before taking that step of restraint. I never imagined myself taking on this type of work, but it certainly prepared me for my future in leadership.

My evolution in consulting included many different responsibilities and tasks, but one that surprised me the most was preparing my client's homes for state inspection. As I spoke with Dionne about it, I joked that I'd become a building surveyor. I was certainly taking on more than I could chew, especially since my client had over ten homes that needed to be inspected in less than three months. The goal was to ensure they passed inspection for annual renewal so that my client stayed licensed in the state. My services included drawing up licensing plans and paperwork needed to conduct the inspections and conducting weekly walkthroughs of each house. Thankfully, Dionne was taking a brief break from her professional career to help me with these inspections. I also provided final write-ups that would go directly to the state. The pressure was immense, but the job was so rewarding, especially because I'd never before been tasked with such a job, nor since. I would've done anything to ensure I maintained my consulting business.

It was a ton of work to put everything together, but being my own boss and managing to pull in a sizable income for the time was an amazing feeling. Like purchasing your first car, you know how much work it is to maintain, but the limits feel endless. You can go anywhere you want, any time you want. And like most first cars, it takes work, time, and money.

No one tells you the intricacies that go into owning your own business, all the little nuances that come from experience and ideally someone telling you what to look out for, such as how to keep going when there's a dry spell of clients and how to market and brand yourself. Even in business school, no one tells you how much of a daily grind it will be to wake up every morning and hustle. While I enjoyed answering only to myself, I hated the hustle. I wasn't a salesperson and found it tough to put a pitch together to gain new business. Because of this, I only ever had two clients, but luckily for me they paid me enough that I never struggled. I became the breadwinner of the household, and soon after starting the business I managed to become debt free and upgrade to a much nicer place with Dionne.

My diving headfirst into relationships did not stop with Dionne. She and I agreed to move in together, and we got a small apartment in North Phoenix, where we settled in with our cats. So much for taking things slow like I thought we would. But it was the first time I felt a real family unit with someone, so I decided then that I would ask her to marry me. I felt I was finally financially capable of providing for us. She quickly became the center of my world, my number one supporter and I hers. She always encouraged me to go after more, and she pushed me to dream big and think about all the possibilities beyond what I could even imagine.

Those moments dreaming with Dionne are some I cherish most. Here was a partner with whom I could bounce ideas around and see the real possibilities that were out there. I felt I was the same blanket of comfort for her; what we wanted to do in the future and who we wanted to become were always similar. She allowed me to think about myself in ways I never could, and I pushed her all the same to hold onto those big dreams she had. We talked for hours about our goals and how we'd strive for them together as a family. For me, it was important we really launch a successful business, so we strategized how we could help it take off. I wanted to build a legacy, and not just for myself but for Dionne and the communities we loved.

Phoenix had become our home, and we found the friendship, community, and belonging we both needed in our lives. Her career had been centered on the performing arts, and her impressive resume included performing on the Broadway stage with the likes of Audra McDonald and Cleo King in shows such as *Ragtime* and *Jelly's Last Jam*. She had been an opera singer and even found herself on stage with the great Leontyne Price (one of the legendary soprano singers of our time). She was a world traveler but was looking to settle in an affordable place where the sunshine was plenty, and she found her way to Phoenix after spending some time in the area for a gig. When we met, she was a struggling artist and I was a struggling careerist, but we somehow found each other. During our time together, she opened a music studio and taught voice lessons, but as time went on she found herself engaged in many other business aspects that took her singing talent to other heights. Then came the desire to act. More to come on that.

While spending time thinking about the bigger picture, I thought one of the ways to make this business grow was to learn from some of the best in the . . . well, business. At the time there was a little-known show gaining popularity called *The Apprentice.* Yes, I'm old enough to remember his ranting and raving about the Central Park Five and his prompting their arrest. He was the epitome of a sham and fraud even in the 1980s. There were several ads on TV and radio seeking a cast for the upcoming season. I brought it up to Dionne, half committed to the idea and wondering whether it would even be worth a try. She actively encouraged me to at least give it a shot: "What's the worst that could happen?"

The day of the casting call, Dionne dropped me off at the convention center and told me to call when I was out. As she sped away, I was met with the longest line of people I'd ever seen, snaked all across the mountain like a never-ending streamer around a Christmas tree. I sheepishly got in the back of the line, already intimidated by the sheer number of people I was competing against for a spot on the show. In my mind, my goal was to meet influential people who'd share their secrets with me on how to run a business. I expected the other people in line to be in the same boat, all of us struggling to make it and hoping to get that one connection that would make everything come together.

As the line started to make some headway, I overheard some people talking.

"So what do you do?"

"Oh, I own an engineering company overseeing over one hundred employees that service the Department of Transportation across the US. What about you?"

"I own a law and accounting firm that manages international business contracts, and I'm based in Abu Dhabi."

"I own a small business consulting agency with two clients here in Phoenix."

I stopped myself from indulging too much when I witnessed the pitiful looks on their faces as I described my business.

Oh no . . . I must be lost.

The more I heard the people around me mingle, the more I realized I was the odd one out. Those who surrounded me in the sea of thousands were certainly doing well for themselves, with budgets ranging from hundreds of thousands to multi-millions and them being at the top of their careers. There I was, surrounded by all of them on top of a hill. I did my best to just keep my head down; I did not want any of them to ask any additional questions about what I did or about my annual salary. Not that they would've noticed anything outside of getting their egos stroked by everyone around them.

I started panicking, thinking about what to do. As the line slowly inched forward, I could feel my heart race faster. *I can't go through with this, right? I'll get laughed out of the audition room by everyone.* Another step forward. *But this could be a great thing. I mean, these moments don't just happen every day.* The line moved up again. *But is it really worth all of this? Everyone here doesn't need this. They just want their fifteen minutes of TV.* The line was starting to round the corner.

As I approached the official check-in, my stomach started to tie itself in knots. I called Dionne on my Nextel phone. "Babe, I need you to pick me up."

"Oh? Is it over?" she asked. "Did you get in?"

"No, I'm still in line. I just can't do this."

"What? What happened?"

"I'll explain later just . . . please come pick me up."

"Okay, well I'll be there soon, okay? Just hold on until I get there."

"Thanks and I love you."

Getting out of a line midway through had never felt so good before. I felt as though an oxygen mask had been placed on my face after finishing a climb to Everest. I started to make my way down the hill, and sure enough, Dionne came quickly to my rescue, saving me from the ego-breathing dragon that was that audition line.

After descending the mountains, we went to grab burgers, and I filled her in on everything. We laughed and agreed that it might be best to hold off on any auditions until we made our first million. It was a learning experience, but one we looked back at fondly. I was grateful to have a partner who understood my dread. At this time in my life, it felt good to know that we would always be there for each other when either of us needed it and would support any decision either of us made. It was an incredible feeling to have someone like her by my side to share these moments with.

Power Couple, Fall 2004

As time went on, Dionne and I became more and more joined at the hip. You couldn't find one of us without the other somewhere nearby, if not literally right next to each other. We started to get a reputation for always being together. Whether it was at our church or some community event, you'd see the two of us. We became the "it couple," the one that seems so perfect it makes other people look at it as the ideal for what they want in a relationship. We supported each other, we cared for each other, and we loved each other deeply.

I loved her and was committed to her, to everything she brought into my life, and with the amount of income I was bringing in, I was able to buy an engagement ring. I picked out the perfect setting for a proposal, a picnic near the place of our first date. On a sunny day, I laid a blanket on the grass and was beaming from ear to ear. After our lunch, I asked her to close her eyes, then reached into my pocket and grabbed the ring. I took her hand and, with her eyes still closed, asked her to marry me. She joked, "I will say yes if I can open my eyes first." She opened her eyes and I asked again, getting down on one knee. A huge amount of relief and happiness rushed over me when I heard her say yes. As if I were floating on clouds, everything felt light, and all I could feel was pure joy. Together, we could do anything.

There was a slight problem with following through on a wedding, however. At the time, Arizona did not recognize same-sex marriages, and they wouldn't fully recognize them for another ten years. In the spring of 2004, Massachusetts became the first to allow them, and the conversation around having more states recognize them was starting to really take shape. This sparked widespread condemnation across the states, with many of them outright codifying bans against same-sex marriages in their state legislatures.

Luckily for us, Phoenix was a blue city at the time, and people were determined to use their voices to be the change the LGBTQ+ community wanted to see in the world. Within the local Phoenix government were conversations about passing an ordinance to at least recognize same-sex relationships as domestic partnerships. Dionne and I didn't hesitate to make sure our voices were heard when it came to the city council meetings and rallying our community behind the efforts to make sure this passed. There were protests held across the state to make sure the legislature heard our voices and to ensure this ordinance passed. With hundreds of other LGBTQ+ people and allies, we and people of all different walks of life and backgrounds marched together to the steps of the capital, demanding this ordinance be put into place.

Rallying together on the steps of the state capitol, with people just like me, was cathartic. All my life I'd hidden because of the fear of retaliation, wondering what someone might say, what someone might do. Growing up, I knew what happened to people who were so visibly out, but this was taking a stand. All our righteous indignation came through each of the chants we all made as one while walking toward the capital. One thing was abundantly clear through all our hearts and voices: We weren't going to just sit and hide anymore, not here and not ever again. If the government wasn't going to recognize our lives, then we were going to make their lives a living hell until they answered to our truth, realizing and seeing us for who we are. Our lives mattered. Our relationships mattered, and they deserved to be not only seen as real but acknowledged as such, a union between two people who love each other regardless of the similarities or differences between them.

Thankfully, the local legislators saw our truth and passed the ordinance in a small but celebratory victory. It brought so much joy and adulation into our lives that Dionne and I celebrated with a commitment ceremony. We were one of the few lesbian couples in the area who held a ceremony after the ordinance was passed, and we were interviewed by *The Arizona Republic* about our ceremony and what it meant to us.

"Why do you think it's so important to hold a ceremony?"

"Because it's important for everyone to know that regardless of who you are or where you come from, you deserve to have the same rights and privileges all straight people have. The ordinance passing was a great step forward, but there's so much more work that needs to be done. This ceremony is just the beginning of a sweeping change that I hope starts to make its way across Phoenix and across the country. Gays and lesbians have always been here, we're not going anywhere, and it's time we start saying it out loud and being proud of who we are."

Throughout the day of our commitment ceremony, October 24, 2004, waves of so many different emotions washed over me. Joy flooded my body as I took the first step down the aisle with my very-soon-to-be wife. Our friends from the church and the local community were all there (even people we didn't want there showed up) to celebrate with us, and they all smiled and cheered for us as we walked down the aisle together hand in hand. As we made our way to the front of the church, I looked into Dionne's eyes and saw my future. Dionne was already more than my wife; she was my flame, my partner, and my life. She saw so much more in me than I could ever see in myself, she helped me discover how to express myself in ways I never knew, and she guided me toward redeeming myself after all the mistakes I made with other people. She also helped me learn how to forgive myself and move forward in a world that felt like it wasn't ready for us. Together we would work to change that.

As we exchanged rings and vows, I looked into her eyes and she looked into mine. We were ready. Putting her ring on her finger, I was committed to her, committed to the love we shared with each other and to growing together as a couple. I loved her and she loved me. As we shared our first kiss together as wives, the audience cheered, champagne bottles opened, doves flew across the sky, fireworks were lit, fighter jets spewed rainbows from their exhaust, and everyone celebrated our marriage. Well, "domestic partnership" in the eyes of Phoenix.

I turned toward everyone, and after feeling like an outsider from so many groups and so many people for so long, I felt like I was home. It was a home that I made, a home with Dionne. This was where I belonged, with a found family and a found peace I never knew I needed and never knew I was searching for.

Coma, Spring 2002

As for my biological family, I never even considered inviting them to be a part of the wedding. I knew what their response would be after what had happened two years prior.

My mom was in San Jose visiting some family and helping take care of a friend. While the details were sketchy at the time, I knew she had been hospitalized after a routine appointment led to a nursing error when they were putting in an IV. They increased her oxygen levels, which caused her body to go into shock, so she was rushed to the hospital and placed in an induced coma for ten days.

Naturally everyone was worried about her, everyone who was told about her condition, that is. Aunt Shirley broke the news to my dad and my siblings, but I was the last person who was brought up to speed on what had happened and what my mom's condition was. One day I just received an out-of-the-blue call from Aunt Shirley: "Kelli, your mom is in the hospital, and we need everyone here. Can you come?"

Upset to hear the news, I replied, "Of course I can!" In the back of my mind, I knew it would be a difficult reunion given I hadn't spoken to my family in eight to nine months. I wasn't sure how to handle the situation, but I booked a flight to be with her, not knowing what to expect.

My uncle, dad, siblings, and aunts were already there by her side when I came bursting through the door, asking every question about her condition, how she was, and what the doctors said. What I didn't expect was to immediately get the cold shoulder from everyone, except my dad. He pulled me to the side and gave me information on Mom's condition.

It was cold in that hospital, especially compared to the warm spring weather outside in sunny California. I felt as if I didn't exist and my family members were hoping that if they did the bare minimum amount of talking to me, I would somehow disappear. That sunk a dagger into my heart, but my first thought was of my mom.

After spending a few hours in the cold and cramped waiting room, the family got a full update from the doctor: "Your mom has fallen into a coma caused by sepsis infection." We were in shock as he spoke. "It could be hours, it could be days," he said. "If she does not come out of this coma after ten days, then the family has a decision to make about next steps."

As I went to be by Mom's side, the words "It could be days" hung over my head like a balloon. I looked over at my mom, and I couldn't help but feel a sense of guilt that if the worst happened, the last time I spoke to her would be out of anger for not being accepted by the family.

That can't be it.

I stared at Mom with pained eyes and watched over her as I listened to the constant ticking of a heartbeat monitor. At least that let everyone in the room know she was still alive. We spent the next ten days in the waiting room of the hospital, hoping the next hour she would open her eyes and everything would be fine. It was agonizing just sitting there waiting and watching for anything that might be a sign she was okay. It was painful enough with just that. But then there was my uncle and the rest of my family.

Anyone who has been given the cold shoulder by a family member knows it's even more gut-wrenching to have it done during a family crisis. At times, I sat alone while the rest of the family prayed or ate together. They talked about Mom's condition and what decisions they had to make as if I weren't in the room—or in the family. The fact that no one else stood up and noticed the obvious resentment from my uncle toward me made my blood boil. Everyone just pretended like it didn't even matter. This was my punishment for my "lifestyle." I was always the different one. I sensed that my dad felt differently.

Dad was more concerned about losing his family prematurely. My being gay didn't stop him from seeing me as his child and as someone he loved and cared for, but he wasn't going to say that out loud, especially there and then. The biggest olive branch he extended was at least talking to me like I was in the room.

After I endured almost a week and a half of the silent treatment, the doctor broke the silence by announcing that Mom was slowly coming out of the coma. We gave my dad a chance to go in first before we each trickled in to see her as she began to open her eyes, relieved that she was back. It was an incredible miracle since the week prior she had been steps away from dying. She looked like she'd woken up from the deepest sleep of her life, which, in a way, was accurate. We were all greeted with a warm smile as she slowly started to gain her senses. Waves of relief washed over us all as we realized she was going to be okay. The doctor soon came in, greeted us all, and told my mom he was glad to see her looking so well after finally waking up. He then cleared my mom and told us she'd be good to go home soon.

I was grateful things were finally looking up, but the scars of the week remained, and I knew nothing had really changed with our family relationships. I was glad my mom had woken up from her coma, but I felt more alone and depressed than I did before. After a few days, it was time for me to head back to my fortress of solitude. With Mom being awake and leaving the hospital with my dad, I knew I couldn't continue holding up the facade that made it possible for me to endure the painful moments of that time with my family.

After leaving the hospital and coming back to Seattle, I made a conscious decision not to interact with my family. If this was how they were going to treat me, if this was what I had to endure just to be around them, it wasn't worth it. If they needed me, they could pick up a phone and call me. I had to carve out my own place for me. So from that moment, I set out to find my people, my tribe who would be there for me when I needed them and wouldn't pretend I didn't exist.

After experiencing the relief that my mom had survived this ordeal, it would take ten years before I would see my family again.

Kelli's Comedy Career, Summer 2005

In the two years following my commitment ceremony with Dionne, my focus shifted to family and ensuring that as the primary breadwinner in the house, I could give Dionne and myself a comfortable life. The rent wasn't going to pay itself, and I didn't have the luxury or time to stop and appreciate what I was building for us. I was always cautiously optimistic about the whole thing. If I stopped working for a week, that was a week money wouldn't come in to pay for food on our table. Dionne was there as a support and a pillar for me, but her primary income was doing community theater and performing at events across the state, so there wasn't a ton supplemental income.

With the constant looming threat of losing income came overworking myself and exhaustion. My health suffered so much that I found myself going in and out of the hospital on a regular basis. There were a series of episodes when I was so dehydrated that I experienced long bouts of vertigo and would pass out. I wasn't a big water drinker, but Arizona heat doesn't care about that. There are days, especially in the summer when it was so hot you couldn't physically be outside. Dionne was confused at first, but panic set in as she witnessed me consistently passing out in my office or in a chair, or worse, with a dizziness that made it impossible for me to drive or walk.

After realizing something worse hadn't happened to me, she'd scold me for not staying hydrated. I always brushed it off. There were more important things to worry about.

Dehydration and worsening inner ear infections were a constant for me for a better part of the year. I had frequent ear infections that I never knew were the cause of why I felt so sick all the time. For months, Dionne and I worried over how to overcome it, and she made it her mission to put me on a strict water regime, which I hated given my disdain for water. She'd say, "Kelli, if you don't drink water, then I am cutting you off!" I had no interest in knowing what I'd be cut off from, so I drank more water. Regardless, every time I went to the hospital complaining of migraines, doctors couldn't figure it out. I got told to get some bed rest, take some Ibuprofen, stay hydrated, all that crap. It wasn't until a doctor started to poke and prod to try to figure out why their repeat customer wasn't getting any better with their great advice that they realized I had an inner ear infection. Luckily they were able to treat it easily with antibiotics, but it's safe to say it wasn't my best year ever for self-care.

During this time, Dionne had an idea that helped me focus on something other than the constant looming anxiety of not having a successful business: my bucket list. Back in early 2003, when I was finally on my own with my own apartment, I'd found myself with more time just for me. Who would've guessed? I spent many days relishing the quiet, the peace that came with being by myself. With peace came new ideas. I started to think about how my life had led to this point, how much more living I wanted to do for no one but me, so I started to write out a list of things I wanted to do with the life I had in front of me, a sort of bucket list. On a yellow legal pad, I wrote down a vision for myself: visiting another country, winning the lottery, writing a novel (I guess you could say I'm scratching that one off the list). I didn't hold myself back, and I dreamed as wildly as I could. I also wrote down that I wanted to do stand-up comedy.

"Hey honey, what's this list?" Dionne asked me. "I was cleaning things up and found this in your desk."

I examined the piece of paper in her hands and smiled, remembering all the things I wrote down years ago.

"Oh, it's like a bucket list. Things I want to do before I, well y'know, kick the bucket." I handed the list back to Dionne.

"Oh? You want to be a comedian?" Dionne looked at me curiously, as if she were sizing me up to be on stage.

"Well, I've been told I have a good sense of humor, and I thought it would be a fun thing to try one of these days." I realized how much people exaggerate but had learned I was funny after all.

"I think you should! You're funny, and I can help you learn the techniques of performing on stage!" Dionne was a true professional in this area. She had spent many years performing on Broadway and then she became a staple on the Phoenix Pride stage. She knew how to command it, and we found she had a small lesbian following who would attend all her Pride shows across the state. I was never jealous, only proud of her talent and charisma.

Meanwhile, I forged my own path toward the stage. In my mind, I thought I could create some jokes and get on stage and that would be that. What I didn't realize was that the first step was a lot more difficult: actually writing funny material. Anyone can write a joke, but making sure the punchline lands and using your body to help carry it were things I didn't even consider until I started to take this idea more seriously.

As any good Aries would do, I threw myself into comedy. I signed up for a comedy class at Scottsdale's once-famed The Comedy Spot and started reading everything I could about comedians and their journeys. In one of the classes, I received training from a comic whose coach was Judy Carter, a famed comic writer who wrote for and with the likes of Robin Williams and several *Saturday Night Live* legends. During the class, I learned techniques for navigating the stage and how to interact with the audience. I also learned how to exaggerate my face and body with a joke and that I shouldn't stare directly into the lights beaming down on the stage but use them as my North Star so I wouldn't fall off the stage. Little technical details an audience doesn't pay close attention to but that help when telling a story and landing a joke. It was like chewing gum and tying my shoe at the same time. *How can I do all this at once?* Weirdly, these tips were the most helpful as I learned how to make this stand-up thing work.

The class was a six-week course, and everyone who participated was tasked with coming up with a set and acting it out in the group so we could give feedback and help each other improve. Every day, I entertained thoughts of how I would start my set. *What could be a punchline to a setup?* I started to look at areas of my life that seemed mundane and ordinary, funny but unfortunate happenings around me that could be added to a set. I bounced ideas off Dionne, and since she was an actor, she helped me rehearse my lines and taught me how to position myself on stage. It was exciting thinking about what I could come up with, and I fell in love with the level of expression, the openness that came with putting myself up on stage and entertaining people. It was an amazing feeling to see my group laugh and to have them help me improve along the way.

The six weeks came and went, and it was time for me to perform. It was June 2005, and I had been in anticipation mode leading up to my first open mic at The Comedy Spot. I knew I had to pack the audience, so I and my classmates invited friends from near and far to join us. Before I knew it, it was time.

My palms were wet. Backstage the comics were drinking like madmen, but since I was a teetotaler at the time, I had downed several ginger ales, which clearly weren't enough. As my music played me onto the stage, I could feel my heart racing. I thought, *Will I get booed off stage and never be able to show myself again?* Then I thought, *I better not, 'cause Dionne and I would lose twenty friends.* As comics based in Arizona, if we all did bomb, we'd at least have the excuse of the extreme heat to explain why we never went outside after embarrassing ourselves.

Suddenly the MC called my name and it was time.

My set was all about people's perceptions of me: "I'm the 'white sheep' of my family."

[Laugher]

"There are three things that make me the white sheep: First, I'm a lesbian—GASP! Two, I listen to country music—GASP!—and three, I recently joined a group with pointy hoods and wear gloves to avoid being recognized. . . . I know. My mother was equally disappointed. 'My baby!'—I exclaimed in imitation as I crumbled to the floor—'Noooo! I never raised you to like country music!' "

[Big laughter]

It was so addictive as I fed off the audience and continued to dig into my set.

I won't put my entire set here, but being able to express myself in this way, seeing people laughing and enjoying the performance I was putting on stage, felt like the most freeing thing in the world. It was cathartic to be able to get on stage and share these personal times in my life with a spin on them and have people be receptive. I didn't have to be anyone on stage other than myself, and people loved it.

My set was only about seven minutes, so I had to try to fit in as many jokes as I could before the end, but by the end and after the set,

I felt an energy I wanted to hold onto. I wanted to keep writing and sharing myself on stage, so I went back to the lab and started to add to my set.

My next opportunity to perform, on and on a bigger stage, came quickly after I heard that a popular comedy reality TV show called *Last Comic Standing*, hosted by Bill Bellamy of *Def Comedy Jam*, was coming to Phoenix for open-call auditions. This was my chance to finally put this set into motion. Would it work? Dionne had so much confidence in me that she helped prepare my material for weeks before the open call. This time I would make it to the front of the line.

Auditions were held at the locally famous venue Tempe Improv where up-and-coming comics were cutting their comedic chops. I figured a handful of people would show up and it would be an in-and-out situation. What I didn't expect was how many people in the area wanted their shots at cracking jokes on TV. The line wrapped around block after block after block, over three times longer than the audition line for *The Apprentice*. People brought tents, food, water, and equipment because they knew they were going to be setting up makeshift homes overnight.

After getting into line (third in place), I got to know the people around me, and I realized how much confidence we all had. We were all anxious and insecure about ourselves, but being on stage brought out a completely different person in all of us. It was an act; we were able to step into the shoes of someone we wanted to be, an idyllic version of ourselves who finally had a voice in the room and with people willing to listen. But at the end of the show when we stepped off that stage, we were still the same anxious and insecure people we were before, hoping some of the act would seep into our daily lives.

Unlike when I was in the other audition linc, I could rclatc to the people who were auditioning with me. Some people had bigger aspirations and were hoping this would turn into a huge opportunity for them to kickstart their career, some just wanted to be on TV, and others like myself just thought it would be a fun thing to try. Regardless of why we were there, we were all a bunch of misfits trying to make people laugh. It was comforting to share our stories with each other and to perform for each other in line, trying to warm up before we got in front of the executives.

Well, we had plenty of time to warm up because people were talking and telling jokes well past 2:00 a.m. I had enough time to go back to my house, shower, and still keep my place in line.

The line chugged agonizingly slow the next morning, but it was finally my time to enter the audition room. Like *American Idol*, each person got five to seven minutes to try to impress the executives in the room, after which they either got their golden ticket or walked home. Walking up the steps, I saw the colorful characters who had shown up to audition, including two clowns and a guy in a chicken costume. *Great*, I thought. *No way they get in, so I must have a chance for this!*

As I walked into the audition room, staff took groups of us at a time and created a "circle of fire." The executives pointed toward one of us and said, "Okay, tell a joke." We formed a circle and performed a round robin of jokes while two rather young producers listened and whispered to each other. It was intense, and we had only one shot to impress the show's producers, even if they looked as though they had just been released from their high school gym class to play producer for the day. I started with my white sheep joke, which elicited big laughs from my peers. It felt good, but it was the producers I needed to impress.

Suddenly we were split into two groups and ushered into our respective rooms. It was clear that at least one group had made it to the next round while the other didn't. It felt like a lifetime waiting in that room. Everyone in my group clenched everything we had, hoping we were the group that made it further into casting.

Through a glass door, we could see the producers walk toward the other group, and shortly after we heard screams of happiness and joy. All the tension in my room disappeared as quickly as I'd heard the screaming, only I couldn't figure out whether I was in the room where it was taking place. I slowly lost consciousness until my brain caught up with my heart and realized I was not in a room of euphoria. All that was left was a bitter feeling of disappointment shared across our group.

We watched the winning group file outside ahead of us, and to my bewilderment the fucking clown and the guy in the chicken costume were in it. *How the fuck did the literal clown and the chicken man perform better than us?!* I couldn't believe it, but the producers confirmed it when they told our group they appreciated us taking the time to come in, but we were not advancing.

None of my group could believe it. These actual clowns were supposedly funnier than us? Talking with everyone, I learned they got accepted because they had an agent or a connection with one of the showrunners. I fumed with anger. "That's bullshit!" I said. "How much time did we spend on our sets, and they get in because they know someone? They weren't even good, and yet we get treated like we're not funny?!"

As usual, Dionne comforted me in my time of need and provided me with the best kiss and hug when I finally slumped into the passenger seat of our car. I left Tempe Improv pissed off, with my confidence shot and me feeling like everything was a sham. It took more than a while to get over the incident, but I wasn't going to let a clown knock me down forever, and I reminded myself why I started doing this in the first place.

The joy that came from making people laugh was enough for me, and after about a month I started to write jokes again. Well, more than just writing jokes again, I seriously committed myself to improving and doing better. Before, I kept an eye out for anything in my daily life that could be made into a joke, and now I was starting each morning with writing jokes about anything that came to mind. Like starting the day with a hot pot of tea, I made sure to never skip a day putting in some effort toward my next set.

Over the next year, I put everything I could into comedy. It wasn't my career, but I made it my mission to constantly improve. I performed three fairly successful sets, and each one taught me more about the craft. I soon began to secure local gigs across Phoenix, including a regular gig with The Comedy Spot in Scottsdale. One day, the owner suggested I check out a gig at a club owned by a relative of a well-known comedian. Only about five comics were allowed to perform there, and each was very much like the comics who tried auditioning for *Last Comic Standing*: praying their careers would take off, hoping to stand out in front of a well-known comic and have a breakout performance. Those thoughts ran through their minds like a spinning wheel. For me, I was signed up by my comedy house owner who thought I had potential. I had no idea what to expect, nor do I think I took it as seriously as those around me.

As I approached the makeshift stage and started to perform as usual, I didn't recognize the asshole in the front row who was apparently a well-known comic at the time. He had made a career as an impressionist and was quite popular, the one everyone else wanted to impress. In the middle of my set after I landed a joke, he said out loud, "That's not funny," and the entire audience burst out laughing. Stunned, I didn't know what to say or do; he was stepping on my set for no reason other than to be an asshole. Every second felt like it dragged on, and all I wanted to do was run off stage.

I finished my set, walked off stage, and didn't have anything else to say. I left immediately and with a pit in my stomach, feeling more pissed off than I did when I left the audition for *Last Comic Standing*. I sat in my car and confided in Dionne about the incident.

"Well he didn't say you weren't funny," she quipped.

"I know. But that's not the point." I couldn't get the moment out of my head. Who was he to say what he did, to walk in and step on me, someone he didn't even know. "I think I'm done. I don't feel like doing this anymore. It's not my ambition, it's not my job, and it's not something I should be this upset about."

Yes, it was one person with one opinion, but something about the way he said it, the arrogance and the tone, made me take a deep look at why I was doing this. It had started as a bucket list item, just something to do that brought me joy, but it was becoming a large part of my life. Now the magic was gone, the veil lifted.

It took a while to remember the whole point of it all. Overall, speaking out and being on stage was a confidence booster and helped me put all of myself in front of a crowd. And I never forgot the power that came with being able to express myself in a way I never experimented with before. There was no need to hold myself back anymore, with anyone.

Chapter 9

Purpose, Direction, and Devastation

Something More, Winter 2007

For the next year, life was good. It felt like I had finally hit that equilibrium, that happy place in life that so many people aspire to reach. My career was going well, and I had a beautifully loving wife and three wonderfully spoiled cats that served as our kids. I started to become more active in business associations in Arizona, and I was starting to entertain the idea of running for public office. I saw doing more for the community, especially for the LGBTQ+ population as the respectability net was widening, as an opportunity to further enhance awareness. There was a ton of goodness on the horizon.

Despite all this, there was always something that kept pulling at Dionne, something she couldn't stop thinking about and was driving her to do more. She'd often hear and regale me with stories about what her acting friends had been up to, the big roles they managed to land, and every time she did I could see the longing in her eyes. She wanted to have the same thing. The idea of stardom never left her mind. We would have conversations more and more frequently throughout the year about moving to LA and her landing a breakout role that would propel her to the front news story of every celebrity gossip show and magazine cover.

There were only two problems with the idea at the time: We were Black, and we were relatively young (in our forties). Hollywood already had a terrible history of catering only to the Whitest people to cast in breakout roles. That still exists today, but at the time they also had a history of casting only younger women who could be sexualized in some way, especially in the late 2000s. You're a thirty-four-year-old White man? Don't worry, you can play a police officer pretending to be a high schooler in a comedy film and no one will bat an eye. You're a forty-year-old beautiful Black woman? Oh. You're playing the witty grandma, and we're going to age you up to fit the role. The latter was a role one of Dionne's friends was constantly squeezed into for different movies she participated in.

Watching someone you love go through audition after audition being constantly rejected, knowing the closest she ever got was for a role where she would've played an aging prostitute, is beyond depressing. But Dionne kept pushing on. It was her dream, and she would try anything to make it happen. I was determined to be there in her corner and see her succeed, even if realistically all I could do was be there to cheer her on. I was there with her through it all and went with her to parties hosted by some of her acting friends. It was at one of them that she started to express her woes and her friend told her what she really needed was an agent. Talking it through with her, I could see the gears turning in her head about how she was going to make this work. Her friend put her in contact with her agent, and they started to have conversations about what this agent could do for Dionne.

The more Dionne described the whole process to me, the more everything sounded great and seemed like it could really work. There was one caveat, though: We'd have to move to LA. Thinking about the memories I had of that place, my heart knew that wasn't where I needed or wanted to be. I felt we had finally found peace in Arizona, and I knew overhauling our lives was going to be a struggle, both financially and for our relationship. Still, I could see the sparkle in Dionne's eyes. She envisioned a move to LA would be a fresh start for her professionally, especially now that she had a decent agent, and everything would come together. Her career would take off, and she'd get record deals and make her mark with a Hollywood star. I could see it written all over her and, as much as my heart protested the idea, I couldn't say no.

Nothing Is Guaranteed

With only a few months to plan the whole move, Dionne and I started to look at locations, trying to keep in mind what would be within our budget and what would be beneficial for her in terms of being close to auditioning sites. She entered an agreement with her new agent, a popular one from Old Hollywood who had been instrumental in helping Late Walter Koenig secure his landmark role as Chekov on *Star Trek: The Original Series*. He wanted to make his client happy, but he did warn Dionne that it might be tough at first, hence the first few roles she auditioned for; there was one where she would've played a prostitute in the now infamous Adam Sandler movie *That's My Boy*. So, rough start, but talk of being on multiple shows and having promising roles was what fueled Dionne and what kept me saying, "That'd be great honey" while I searched for new job prospects of my own in the area.

She eventually landed a role as character actor on a few Conan O'Brien shows, which gave her some exposure. When I finally met her agent and a few of his famous clients, I was struck by the rather somber tone of the holiday party we'd been invited to. I was more intrigued by our other famous friends, namely Cleo King who had a small but memorable part in the widely popular film *The Hangover*. She and Dionne had reconnected when we made the decision to move to LA, and we became a staple of many house parties where I met up-and-coming Black artists from all walks of life. My favorite was mingling with comedians, including Leslie David Baker (Stanley from *The Office*) and Kym Whitley (Monina from *Curb Your Enthusiasm*). I was impressed by their stories of perseverance as they worked hard to get to the place where they were known by more than their faces. They were starting to become household names. It was this part of the Hollywood scene that made me feel comfortable—seeing my people rise above their White counterparts and "make it big."

With such a short amount to pack up our lives and our furry kids, I said my goodbyes to our closest friends and colleagues. We left quite a big mark in Arizona, and that was something I still look back at fondly. It didn't start well, and I didn't come back into in the best state of mind either time. But I was leaving doing more than I thought I ever would and with more confidence in myself this time. I knew who I was, and I wasn't going to let that hold me back.

With tearful goodbyes and promises we'd keep in touch, being only a state away from each other, Dionne and I loaded up a truck and drove across state lines. As I looked back when we were leaving our home, I could only hope that things would be all right, that somehow we'd make it. I'd always managed to find a way, even in the most desperate situations. I'd always been able to find some foothold and pull myself back from the edge of the sheer cliff of life. *Who knows? Maybe Dionne's career will really take off and I can take more time for myself.* Those thoughts kept racing through my head all the way across the desert.

We settled in the City of Torrance, south of LA. It was one of the actual livable areas in the area that was close enough to the city but just outside the dense population. We were able to find an apartment while we started to search for new job prospects. As soon as we parked the truck in the driveway, we hit the ground running.

Living in California was pricey (go figure), and we had only the savings I'd accrued from my business. It was enough to get by and pay rent for at least a few months, but we weren't going to make it long after that without something to support us. I started to apply for any training or supervisor jobs available because those were the positions in which I was most comfortable and accomplished, yet I was turned down or didn't receive a return call from every role I applied to. Day after day, it felt like things were slipping through our fingers. The grand promises of Dionne's agent didn't materialize as quickly as he expected, and she was still struggling to land any big gigs or roles that would help bring in the income we needed. Both of us were struggling week after week, and Dionne had to start driving back to Phoenix to take on some gig work to bring in something for the two of us. A lot of the work she did in Phoenix, such as theater shows, vocal lessons, and performing workshops, were seasonal, so it was either feast or famine. Since she had to travel back and forth between Phoenix and LA, it barely allowed us to keep our heads above water. She'd be gone for days at a time, leaving me to contemplate what I was going to do and what other job opportunities were available to me.

After a few months spent spinning our wheels, we were lying in bed one night, both of us anxious about our situation. We had given up everything to be here, including the comfort of our home, our social circles, and our community. What was it all for if we were just going to keep spiraling downward?

When the silence became deafening, I turned to Dionne and said, "Listen honey, we either need to leave LA or something else because I don't know how long we can keep doing this."

Dionne stayed silent. I could see the anxiety on her face in the dimly lit room. She didn't want to admit it, that all of this was such a huge gamble, that we had given up everything to be here only to fall flat on our asses.

"I know . . . I just . . . I thought this would be easier being over here, y'know?" She looked over at me, hoping to have some comfort.

I met her eyes. "I know, but the reality is, we're not going to make it if we keep going like this. Something's going to have to change."

She nodded her head. Both of us knew the ship was sinking; this was our *Perfect Storm* moment with neither of us wanting to abandon ship after having given up so much. We were in too deep, and neither of us wanted to quit.

A few days later, a ray of light broke through our storm. I got a call back from an employer for a senior consulting position for a prominent hospital in LA, Kaiser Permanente. I was euphoric about the potential to work for the largest medical system in the country. Working for this hospital was the jackpot, and the weight and the prestige associated with working for them, let alone the free healthcare, made it a very coveted position, the running joke being you needed to work there to be able to afford the insurance.

Upon hearing the news that I was selected for an interview, I felt like I was going to be able to breathe soon. I brought all the luck and confidence I could muster to that interview. Well, several interviews. Getting in with this hospital felt like being interviewed by the CIA. They scoped out every aspect of my life to make sure I was the right one, and every time I talked to Dionne after an interview, she asked with anxious enthusiasm how everything went. After every interview, I said I thought it went well but left only with the promise that they'd look over everything that was said and get back to me.

Four rounds of interviews and four months later, I received the call I had been waiting for. I could not feel any lighter, and my mind was swimming in the clouds. The air felt cooler, the water tasted better, and the smog that usually covers LA felt a little more breathable. Well, minus the smog part. I could not have been happier to land this position. Granted, it paid a bit less than what I was making back in Phoenix, but it was at least something. Dionne and I could soon stabilize and start thinking about more than when rent was due.

The hospital's mission was to ensure everyone had the capacity and ability to receive healthcare. Aside from the paycheck, their mission statement was the key to my longevity. I believed in helping all communities but especially those most underrepresented. They wanted to create something more for their employees and to do what they could to support the communities around them. It was something I seriously aligned myself with, and I had an extremely supportive boss who helped push me in the right direction.

My boss was a critical care unit nurse, and she helped give me ideas on training programs that were lacking at the time. She trusted me and gave me a lot of opportunities to start to flex the career muscles I'd built up as an educator and consultant. I brought in several different programs, one popular one being a new nurse preceptorship for incoming student nurses. Being that I was a non-clinical educator, this was the type of leverage I needed to up my game and boost my confidence that I could build something from the ground up. I was anxious yet excited to get started, and after many months in the development phase, a program was born. It was a preceptorship program where nursing students received on-the-job training from nurses in hospitals, a common training program for students who sought to become qualified nurses within our health system. It was prestigious and sought out by so many students that it was often difficult to catch up with what I had worked to build, but it was coming along. Once it launched, I received kudos from my boss and the nursing department.

The news traveled fast and I was making waves, becoming much more visible with the development of each program. I was starting to get my hands into several different areas of the hospital. It felt good to be recognized, especially as a woman in this role, let alone a Black lesbian, which wasn't something out of the ordinary in the early 2000s. There were few Black lesbian women who were rising through the administrative ranks as quickly as I was.

The work I was doing was widely celebrated, and I was in touch with my intersectionality as well as building friendships and alliances with other women of color. It was during this time that I was asked to join employee business groups, and one in particular took my life in a different direction. I joined our LGBTQ+ Alliance group to address gender-affirming care and gender identity advocacy for both employees and patients throughout Southern California. I scored the secretary position and found myself at the forefront of a movement that elevated LGBTQ+ health in a way I never imagined I'd be a part of. Our first line of business was to work toward addressing and honoring gender identity by introducing pronouns in medical health records and gender confirmation surgeries throughout our health systems across the region. It was revolutionary work at the time, and I was right in the middle of it. It was the most inspired and complete I felt since coming out of the closet all those years earlier.

On top of my side gig with the employee resource group, my day job kept me busy as well. I was responsible for overseeing new employee orientations, which was where I shined. Every month or so, I spent three or four days in front of thirty to forty new fresh faces, helping them get acclimated to their new world and one of the hottest spots to work at the time. Those days were some of the most rejuvenating of each month. I'd stand in front of a large crowd of new hires and have a chance to use my style of comedy to lighten up the room and bring some excitement to what otherwise would've been perceived as a one-time training that might be forgotten once a trainee starts their new job. I made every attempt to make it a memorable week for these new Kaiser employees. With my style of comedic presentation, I was able to relate to new hires with my own stories of how I stated my career, where I'd come from, and what I wanted to do now. I was really in my element!

Those moments solidified what I wanted to be doing as a career. As I taught and expounded upon the experiences I'd had and the experience many of the new employees would have, I learned more about what was really important to me in this career. In almost every job I'd had before, I was scraping by, making things up as I went, or really just doing it for the paycheck. While I loved having my own business, this new position gave me a different sense of purpose, and I had a chance to really make it more than just a survival gig. There was something more to all the success I had thus far, and I was eager to do more.

I was moving into the position of leader and starting to see the impact I could have on people's lives. I wanted to leave my mark on something, to do something more for myself and for other people than just scrape by. I wanted to give people some hope that they could excel in any position. I didn't have any leaders or inspirational people who looked like me so I had to become that person. And I wanted to be that person for those younger than me.

After each session, I always asked for feedback from the groups about anything I could improve on and things they thought were great. Every time, I consistently got great feedback and reviews about the stories and experiences I shared. People felt connected to me and would remark how comfortable they felt opening up about their experiences. Hearing the glowing reviews strengthened my commitment to do better for those around me, and it also helped build my confidence and lower my therapy bills. I was thriving as an out, Black, professional woman who was helping uplift all the communities surrounding me.

Achievement, Spring 2011

With more of my work getting recognized, I was put on a fast track of promotions, until I hit the proverbial glass ceiling. I was on track to becoming a director, but there was one thing standing in my way: my lack of advanced education. Kaiser Permanente required all its management and leaders to have at least a master's degree. I wasn't going to let that stop me, and after learning that I'd be on the track, I decided to continue my education. I started to take online classes during the free time I had, and I buckled down to get my master's as quickly as I could.

As it turned out, when I had a goal and the commitment to see this through, I excelled in my classes, consistently turning out near-perfect scores on essays and tests. What I had lacked so much in my first attempts at college was the discipline to sit through classes and start to absorb the material. Even more so was an idea of what I was going to achieve with the degree. After graduating from high school, college felt like a natural extension. The general mindset was, *We're young, we don't understand what the world is going to look like when we graduate or what we even want to do in life, so we take a lot of it for granted. Some of us find a way through it, while others require more time and experience.*"

Within a year and some change of starting my MBA, I finished the requisite number of classes and credits to receive my degree. Knowing I'd soon have a master's degree and be promoted to the position of director, I felt like I was achieving everything I knew I wanted so many years ago. I had a direction for my life and was thriving in my job. Everything was lining up, and I needed to spread the word of my successes.

With my graduation date set, I started to prepare the announcements. Friends and colleagues were equally excited to see a master's degree with my name on it, and Dionne constantly sent me affirmations congratulating me on all the work I'd done up to this point. In a way, all of this was the culmination of decades of work and self-improvement, not just professionally but also personally, and I couldn't be happier to soon be on the other side of it.

There were just a few other people I considered inviting to the ceremony: my family. I hadn't spoken to them since Mom's near-death experience, they never sent any sort of card or email making sure I was doing all right. Still, I wrote them a long email detailing everything I'd been doing and how I would soon receive my master's degree and would like them to see me graduate.

I didn't know what to expect. A part of me wished I'd get some sort of congratulations; even a one-word message back would at least acknowledge they saw the letter. Clearly, they were going to miss one of the biggest days of my life and while disappointing, it wasn't too surprising, but at the age of thirty-eight, I'm not sure what I could've expected from them at this point.

The day finally came, and my anticipation grew with every hour leading to the drive to the stadium. Dionne helped me get ready and noted where she'd be in the audience. The ceremony commenced, and I was so proud to have my closest friends there, some who traveled to see me, which brought joyful tears. As I eyed the stands back and forth looking for any sign of my family, I saw the one person who made my life complete and always believed in me: Dionne. Without her I never would've thought this day could be a reality. She made everything whole, and I was proud she was by my side. It allowed me to take a deep breath and exhale.

Row by row, we were called up to the stage. Finally my name was called, and all I could hear in a sea of supporters was Dionne and my friends cheering me on. I gave a slight smile as I walked across the stage and shook the hands of the faculty. Even through the disappointment at the thought of my parents not being part of such a pivotal moment in my life, I knew I hadn't done all this work for them. This was never about making someone else happy or proud of me. All I could do now was be proud of myself and the work I'd done to be there at that moment. I looked into the camera, posing with the culmination of my life over the past two decades.

I was the first person in my family to receive a master's degree, and the day was one of the most gratifying moments of my life.

I'd spent hour after exhausting hour during brutal days of work to achieve this. I'd proven to myself, more than anything, that I was going to accomplish more than going to a trade school. I may not have been accepted nor graduated from prestigious schools like my siblings had, and no expectations were ever placed on what I'd do with my life, but there I was, shaking hands with the dean, with a crowd of people who all loved and supported me. It may not have been my family or my parents, but it was something I'd created. And no one can take that away from me.

Annihilation, Summer 2011

The summer after I graduated, Dionne and I were fully settled into our new home outside of LA. She could see I was stressed out about not speaking to any of my family after about seven years. Even after graduation, I never got a peep out of my mom, nor any of my family. Not a congratulations, let alone a "Hope you're well." Except for one person. The only one who called me consistently, every day, was my dad. He was the one who truly and deeply cared about me. He left me voicemails and gave me quick and straightforward updates on all that was happening in Reno, and he always ended them with "Call your mom."

That last line was what always put me off from talking to him, from ever picking up the phone. I knew that the second I called, he'd hand over the phone to my mom, and then it would turn into a larger ordeal. So I constantly avoided it. I avoided every call he made. I felt they were all bait to get me to talk to my mom. I listened to my dad's voicemails and got caught up on how people were doing and whether someone passed away, but I could never bring myself to send him a message back. As nice as it was to know he cared, I knew so much of it was about wanting to bring me back into good graces with my mom.

As the days went on, Dionne could see the stress continuing to mount on me. Tensions were mounting between the two of us too. More and more, she was gone days at a time for work, leaving me to stew at home. Trying to reconcile what to do, Dionne suggested maybe it would be helpful to hear from my family. To hear from my mom.

I sat with the thought for a while. I knew this was going to come up one day. As I picked up the phone, every part of my body tried to brace itself for the disappointment to come.

My mom sounded so excited at first. "Oh my baby! It's great to hear from you."

My body reflexively started to turtle up as if I were again a kid under the benevolence of her parents. "Hey, Mom, good to hear from you too."

Conversation quickly went to missed calls and responses. She'd mention something about it, and I'd sheepishly say, "I know, I know . . ."

I tried to address the elephant in the room and said, "Hey, so I sent you an invitation for my graduation. I got my master's degree!"

I could feel the tone shift in her voice. "Well we got your invitation, but you know we couldn't come out there."

"I know."

"Well you know, I don't like how you've taken the direction of your life."

"I can't believe you're so dismissive about these accomplishments."

"I'm not going to go to hell because you're gay."

"What does that mean?"

"I don't want to go to hell because of your lifestyle, which I do not support."

I pulled the phone away from my ear and looked at it. I stopped listening while she was going on a long-winded religious tirade. *Hit the End Call button*, I thought. I threw the phone down, furious. After all this time, after everything. I'd attempted to finally become the best version of myself only to be torn down by the people I love. It was hurtful and sent me into an immediate spiral.

I don't know whether she even knew I hung up on her. She probably finished her rant, nodded her head, and pretended like she had some impact on me by putting me on "God's path" again. I knew this was how she was going to show up. I can get a good read on people and what their reactions are going to be by watching their behaviors. My gut instinct told me this was never going to be a good idea, and lo and behold, I got exactly what I expected. This was why I never answered, why I never called. In the course of ten minutes, I realized I didn't really have a family anymore.

After that, I could only put one foot in front of the other and hold onto what I did have: Dionne, my career, and this $100,000 piece of paper that said I could now advance in my career.

❧ ❧ ❧

While my career was taking off, Dionne's was not. It had been years since moving to LA now, and all the fancy promises about the glitz and glamour of Hollywood were finally showing for what they really were: promises only for the select few lucky enough to catch a break. The roles promised to Dionne never materialized, and she was struggling to figure out where to take her career. She tried everything she could, but nothing would stick in LA. The industry was moving quickly, and roles she could star in today didn't exist yet.

What did come up for her consistently was gig work back in Arizona. All of a sudden, and after having gotten my master's degree, we were having conversations about moving back to Arizona.

"Are you serious? We moved out here for you, and now you're thinking of just, what?! Packing it all up again and moving back?" I couldn't do the same thing again.

Dionne crossed her arms and said, "I know it's a lot, but I need to try to find work for myself as well. I mean, I can see what happens. Maybe some things will change, but for right now my career is in Phoenix."

I took a deep breath. "We'll see what happens," I said, "but if you need to do this more consistently then go, because I also have a career here now."

And go was what she did. What started out as a trip out to Phoenix every three months or so soon became every two months, then every month, then weekly. Every week, she was gone from the house days at a time for some new gig work in Phoenix, and more often than not I came home to an almost empty home. "Almost," on account of our three cats, who kept me company whenever I returned from work or woke up in the morning.

The more often Dionne left, the more I felt the strain on our relationship. We weren't communicating well with each other about what both of us wanted. We just kept things going as is, and conversations between us became shorter when she was away on her trips. When she was around, I noticed little things in her behavior seemed to have changed. She seemed a lot more secretive and selective about what she told me when she was away. What used to be long tales of what happened and the drama of it all became like asking a kid how school was. "It was fine," they say before focusing on picking at their dinner. She wouldn't use her phone around me but would go to the bathroom to use it, and when I confronted her about it she'd say, "Well I need my privacy." I felt annoyed but even more suspicious. She never used to do these kinds of petty things around me before. Why now? Every question I asked was met with a dodged response or evasion. It was chewing away at me from the inside, and I didn't want to believe the worst-case scenario was real.

One night, I found she had left her email open on the computer back at our home and noticed she'd been talking to someone quite frequently. I scoured some of their conversations and didn't see anything incriminating, but it was definitely a lot more suspicious than just two friends or coworkers emailing each other back and forth.

Our plan was for me to come visit her during her gig on a Disney cruise ship once it docked at a port in Miami, and I had already thought about how I was going to confront her about this.

As I was making my way up the loading ramp, swarms of kids were leading the charge with their parents trying to catch up, and heading the opposite way was a giant Stitch mascot from *Lilo and Stitch*. I tried to keep my focus, but Stitch spotted me and, of course, charged directly at me after bypassing the kids.

"You want a hug?!"

"No! I don't need a hug." I was a grown-ass woman who was on a Disney cruise. No hug necessary.

"You look like you need a hug!" Stitch said, forcing me into a hug to the cheer of all the kids around me.

Great. Already off to a shitty start.

Little did I know I was going to need that hug after all.

I met Dionne, and we were happy to see each other since she'd been gone for a while on this cruise. I waited until we were alone and at a good enough time to confront her. We got to her room, and I brought up the email thread. "Sooo who's this person you're talking to?"

Dionne looked for something to latch her eyes onto. "Oh they're just a friend from Philadelphia," she said.

I knew I was onto something, and I blurted out, "Is she gay?"

"Well yeah, but it's all right, it's just friendly." I could tell she didn't want to make eye contact.

"You talk to this person so much more intimately than you do to me. That doesn't seem like it's just friendly."

Dionne got up and looked me in the eyes. "Kelli, listen. You're just projecting, okay?! You're thinking way too much about this. She's just a friend. Now can you drop this, and can we enjoy this night?"

"Fine."

Our conversations always seemed to end like this. She'd get more and more defensive, yet we carried on like usual. That's how it went this time as well. We carried on the rest of the night like we always had, as if there weren't anything bad going on between the two of us. We were both buried underneath the professional masks we now wore.

For the next month, things kept going like this, though I was able to put on the look of a leader at work without any of the home-related nightmare seemingly bothering me. I was good at masking, and work gave me something to focus on other than Dionne. I was able to continue excelling at what I was doing, and I always committed myself to taking on more when needed.

A few weeks later at a friend's house party, I began to open up about the troubles I was facing at home. I'd confronted Dionne multiple times, but I had no idea what to do about it.

They took all of it in and told me, "Well, it sounds like what you need is something definitive, something she can't refute against you, y'know?"

"Yeah, but everything I've tried hasn't led to anything. I don't know what I can do."

They took a moment to think, then said, "Well, can you take her phone when she's sleeping or something?"

A light bulb went off. "We share a phone plan together, and I can see her call history."

"There you go. Check that and see who she's calling. Then you bring that up to her. That's something she can't deny."

I nodded my head. This was the last thing I could do to confirm whether I was being paranoid or gaslit.

When I came home, I started to scour Dionne's phone records, and I saw one number that was called every day. I couldn't see any of the text message history, but I decided to call the number. With every button I pressed, I started to sweat, and while waiting for someone to pick up, I felt rage swell up inside me. It wasn't long before a woman answered the phone.

"Who is this?" I heard from a soft voice on the other side of the phone.

"Well, this is Kelli. Who's this? Looks like you've been calling my wife every day. Do you have an answer?"

There was nothing but silence for a few moments, then "Well, you have to talk to her about that."

Click.

I fucking knew it.

I could feel the rage and anger creating a storm inside me. All this time, all those trips. I knew I wasn't going crazy with what I was seeing. I'd done everything for her at every turn. Whenever she needed something, I was there to help provide it. Whenever she wanted something, I was there in her corner to help support her. What the fuck was it all for? What was the point of moving to LA, uprooting our entire lives, if this was what she was going to do?

I needed to hear her say it. I needed to know it was the truth, and I needed to hear it from Dionne's mouth. Unfortunately, or fortunately for her, she wasn't there to face retribution. She was gone for the week and wouldn't be back for a few days.

I couldn't stay in that house while she was gone, so I went to stay with a friend while I stewed and sat in the ugly truth. All I could think about was why. Was it something about me, or was it the situation? What compelled her to do this?

She came back on a Monday, and I didn't hold anything back. "What the fuck is this?" I said while pulling up the phone records and showing them to her.

She looked defiantly at me. "What are you talking about? So we're doing this now?"

"No, I called her and asked her who she was. Her response was to ask you, so now I'm asking you. Who is she?"

I could see her carefully thinking about her next words. "We're just friends, okay? She may want more from me, but she's also a part of the church, so I see her every time I go back to Phoenix, okay?! There's nothing more to it than that."

I couldn't believe she'd deny it even now. "So that's it, then?! You just talk to her constantly, every day, and there's nothing more? You honestly expect me to believe that?"

"I don't know what else to tell you, Kelli." As she walked off, she cooly added, "Anyway, I have to go back for another event on Wednesday, so I'm only here for a few more nights."

Of course she was. She was off to run away again with another woman.

I didn't know what to do. I didn't know whether to kick her out, whether to scream or cry. I let her stay that day, but the next day while she was gone I packed up all her things in boxes. I marked them with her name and her so-called friend's name, then left them in the garage for her to find when she came back.

There wasn't any discussion a week later when she returned to find all her things packed up. She silently picked them up, put them in her car, and drove off. All I could do was watch as she pulled out of the driveway. There she went after everything we'd been through, after all I had been through. She just left. We were trailblazers, and now we were broken. I balled my hand in a fist and screamed.

Unfortunately, there's rarely a clean breakup that allows you to heal. Dionne never admitted it was the truth, and something in me wanted to believe in her, to take her back, to not believe that all we'd been through was for naught.

August 5, 2011

Months later, I learned that Dionne had been living in Phoenix with this mystery woman, but that didn't stop me from attempting to reach out to her via calls and texts. I needed answers. When she did answer, her responses were short and hurtful.

I ended up calling a church friend of Dionne's, an older gay woman she adored, and during that call, I pleaded with her as if I were on my hands and knees, desperately asking for any information on Dionne.

"Well, Dionne doesn't want to be with you," she said flatly. "You have to let her go. If she's willing to be in the burning-hot hell of Phoenix rather than with you, then she's not the person for you."

I hung up the phone with intense rage. I couldn't believe it. I didn't want to believe it. How could this woman, the love of my life, treat me so abhorrently? I needed to know, no I *had* to know what was real, and I couldn't let her go. She was my everything.

A few days later, I got a hold of Dionne. I didn't have a moment to plead my case. The second she heard my voice, she admitted it without me having a chance to say anything. She couldn't keep it a "secret" any longer. Everything was now confirmed as the truth. She had met someone back in Phoenix who was always there in the background during every performance Dionne was a part of and had started talking to her. The more they talked, the more intimate the relationship between them became. One thing led to another, and Dionne formed an attachment that eventually led to infidelity.

As I heard her talk about it, the blood rushed out of my head and my body felt limp. I wasn't in control of my emotions, my thoughts, or my body; everything was on autopilot. I could only watch as a passive observer while my soul was being thoroughly crushed underneath the weight of the truth. I didn't know what to say. What do you say when the woman who's been with you through so much of your life, the one you've given up so much for, says she has cheated on you?

"I can't be with you anymore." Her words sounded so cold I could feel them send a shiver across my whole body. This was it. This was the end. There was nothing left here for me. I didn't want to do this anymore. I didn't want anything anymore. What was the point of trying? What was the point of living?

I hung up the phone and needed to turn my brain off. I didn't want to think anymore. I didn't want to confront the reality I was living in. I started to walk toward the garage, making sure all the exits were sealed. I was a passive observer as my body acted on its own. I wished the pain away. I didn't want to care anymore. I sat in the car and turned it on. I figured I would sit there and wait for whatever happens when you die. I just hoped it would come quickly so the racing thoughts would stop. Hopefully it would be like a dream and I'd wake up in heaven, happy I left the world.

Carbon monoxide started to fill up the garage, and I could smell it coming in from the air vents. This was it. My final moments wouldn't go out with a bang, with a weeping crowd of loved ones by my bed side. They would find me locked in my car. IF someone found me.

As I shut my eyes and waited to pass out, something in my head grew louder and louder, some small part of me that wouldn't be silenced by my despair, that wanted some way out of this insanity. "Call Amira," it said loudly. "Call Amira right now!"

Amira was a coworker and close friend who knew a lot about my situation and what I'd been going through over the past couple of months. In our time working together, we'd formed a strong bond, and that small part of me knew Amira may have some sort of answer. I looked down at my hands and noticed my phone was there with me. Strange. I didn't remember taking it with me. It was almost like it had been planted there by someone else.

I slowly dialed Amira's number and waited for a response. This was the real moment. This would decide what my fate would be. If she answered, then clearly I was meant to live. And if she didn't, well . . . I'm able to write this now because of her. She answered the phone very casually, thinking nothing of the phone call until she heard my voice. "Amira, I need help."

She could hear the raspiness in my voice as I realized she actually answered. "Kelli? What's wrong? Are you okay?" I could hear how concerned she was. It felt like the first time someone was actually concerned for me in decades.

"I'm in my car in the garage . . . and I have the car running."

There was a pause before she responded clearer in tone, trying to hold back a shaky voice. "Okay, I need you to turn off the car first of all. Can you do that?"

My body started to move on its own. There was no arguing; Amira was now the one in control of my body, and all I could do was follow instructions. I turned off the ignition and said, "Okay, it's off."

A sense of relief took over Amira's voice, knowing I was at least going to be okay for right now. "Okay, now, I need you to open the garage. Can you do that?"

"Yes." I shuffled out of the car and opened the side door, letting the noxious fumes escape along with my darkest thoughts. As the door opened, there were police standing outside waiting for me. Amira had managed to call the nonemergency line while I was completing my tasks.

"Ma'am, are you okay? Are you trying to harm yourself?" one of the officers asked me, extending a hand as if to help pick up a small child.

Amira reassured me, "It's okay, I called them to help. Please take their help, Kelli."

"Yes, I was trying to hurt myself." I could respond only with a sense of helplessness and embarrassment.

The officer stepped forward like he was approaching a wounded animal and asked, "Would you like to take a ride to get some help?"

I could only nod my head before the officer gently guided my hand and my body toward the police cruiser. While I sat in the back seat, I let Amira know I was okay. "I'm going to get help."

With a relieved sigh, she said, "Okay, Kelli. I'm glad you're okay, and I'm glad you called me."

I stared blankly ahead of me at the backseat of the cop's car before some semblance of my mind came back to my body. The officer informed me that by law he had to handcuff me "for my safety." As I felt my hands being placed behind my back and heard the click of the handcuffs, I suddenly realized that this was my life now. All I could think of was the last thing Amira said to me as I was being taken in.

"Amira?"

"Yeah?"

"Thank you."

"You're welcome, Kelli. I'll talk to you soon."

Chapter 10

Recovery

Rebirth, August 5–8, 2011

I was escorted by police into the detainment center, where I slept overnight on the floor with a small pillow and tattered blanket before being assigned to a treatment facility. The detention center was overcrowded, sticky, and stunk of pee. It was cold, but everything felt numb. I was still in a daze over what had just happened, and my suicidal brain had moved into thoughts of reflection. After spending nearly a decade with this person, I was prepared to kill myself because I lost her. And now, there I was at a detention facility in a room filled with strangers, all there for various reasons.

The next morning I was taken to a facility by ambulance, another surreal experience. They checked me in and allowed me one phone call to anyone, and I was given a journal when I entered. The person who checked me in explained the rules of this space. There was an outside area for residents (as we were called) to enjoy, and we were never confined to one room at a time during the day. Lights out and restrictions on leaving our room were at 9:00 p.m. We had little access to anything other than what they provided and what they allowed us to hold onto at certain times. The whole facility was like a weird resort. The space was calm, but I could see no one was there for vacation, even though it had a pool table and a library. Some people were admittedly "crazy" (their words, not mine) and some were seeking help, while others looked calm and just wanted to be alone. We were all paired with roommates. Thankfully, mine was very calm, but she was suicidal (her words). I could relate after what I'd just been through, but by the time I was in the facility, I was starting to come out of the trance I felt I was in when I walked into my garage.

It was a sobering experience, like spending a week at the Betty Ford Clinic. There was the system shock of joining and being in there for the first few moments, but the more time went on, the more I felt my senses start to return to my body. I felt the weight of my actions that put me in here in the first place and resolved to make sure I didn't end up back here again.

I started to write in the journal they gave me, beginning by writing my name and the title "Rebirth." I'd been given a second chance, which told me I was meant to be here for something more, and I wasn't going to give this life for someone ever again. God had given me a new plan, and this experience only strengthened my resolve to keep walking forward.

Journaling my thoughts and recording what happened helped calm my nervous system. I was able to start breathing again and calming my heart. I started journaling about my future, what I wanted to do in the short term, and what things I wanted to achieve in the long term. The first goals were to take a real shower and change my clothes. Continuing therapy was my second short-term goal, and it's something I've stuck with to this day.

As I started to think and write about my long-term goals, I knew I needed to find a new home. There was a lot I knew I needed to do, but there was also a lot I wanted to do. Traveling across the globe, living in a foreign country, and writing this memoir were on both my long-term and short-term lists. The last long-term goal I wrote down was to make a difference on this Earth.

I also started journaling about Dionne and our relationship. The time spent with her was always going to be a part of me, and the simple pleasures of the life we shared together are the ones that felt the hardest to lose. The home we shared was gone, but the happy moments we had together, the waves we made together, are things that will never change and can never be taken away from me. I grieved over what was, but she had made her decision, and I had to make mine going forward. I needed to focus on what *I* could do now, on what was in front of me and what I could do to help myself heal. Emotional turmoil and pain are things that are never "cured" in the span of a few days or with only one or two therapy sessions. Scars stay with us for our entire lives, but the healing comes from the continual work we put into ourselves each and every day.

By the third day, a psychiatrist came in to review my case. It was essentially a review about my mental health and the events leading up to my attempt. She came in, sat across from me, and said, "Well, in looking over your file, we do not believe you have any further suicidal ideologies."

"Well I don't. I was distressed over the breakup with my wife and attempted to harm myself in relation to that."

She nodded. "Okay. I'm going to ask you a couple more questions. Do you feel you would harm yourself again?"

"No."

"Do you feel you suffer from depression?"

"Yes, I believe I do."

She nodded again. "We recommend that you see your therapist after this, but we'll be releasing you by noon today."

I breathed a sigh of relief. I didn't know how long I'd be in the facility and was glad it wouldn't be much longer.

After checking out, I made multiple promises to myself. A lot of them were about giving myself grace as I moved through this time in my life, staying positive and trying to remain optimistic about my future, and keeping up with therapy and counseling. I sought a more specialized therapist to help me with my depression, but all in all, I knew the next couple of months were not going to be easy. There was a lot that needed to be done, but stepping out of the facility with a renewed sense of self was the first step toward recovery.

Exit Strategy, Summer/Fall 2011

Those three days I was in the facility were the only ones I took off without fanfare. For all everyone knew, I had finally decided to take some time for myself and live a little. The following Monday, I walked back into the office like nothing had happened and went back to work as usual, even though I knew everything had changed.

I followed up with Amira, and she was relieved to hear I was okay. It was a relief to know there was someone out there with whom I could share the experience, good or bad. I'm forever grateful she answered the phone when I needed it. We're still friends to this day, but I kept this hidden from others, especially those from work. It's something that happened, and the last thing I needed was everyone asking questions or treating me differently.

I found a specialized psychologist, and we talked through my life experiences and my bout with depression. It was good to have those sessions, and they helped tremendously, but being in the environment, in LA, I couldn't get Dionne out of my head. It was codependency at the highest level, and I was sucked into hours scrolling through her Facebook profile and staring at all the things she was doing, seeing her in a new relationship while they enjoyed their lives together. It was heartbreaking. I couldn't explain why I had become so fixated. Honestly, I'm surprised I didn't fall into a deeper depression because of it. But a deep part of me was determined never to be put back in the facility because of someone else.

I hated that I was becoming the type of person who'd snoop constantly, who couldn't let go of her ex, but that's what codependency does to you. My connection to Dionne remained intensely part of my life, and even after my attempt there was a piece of my heart that always wanted her back. I desperately wanted to revive the happier times, to have the fairy-tale ending with her that's in every cheesy '80s rom-com movie.

Unfortunately, real life isn't a movie. It works in ways we never completely understand. I don't remember how, why, or when exactly it happened, but I got my wish. In October Dionne came back into LA from Phoenix for work. She still had big aspirations of being a star, and on one of those trips we reconnected.

Dionne told me she was confused about why she had left me to be with another woman given the love we shared. Apparently, the other person was very into church, which was something Dionne valued heavily. In our relationship, she was upset over the amount of time I wasn't spending at and giving to church. She wanted to be with someone who'd pour themselves into the institution, and she found that kinship in this other person. The caveat to that relationship was that she was a huge pot smoker and Dionne hated it. She hated having the house filled with smoke all the time and finally had enough. She said our breakup was a mistake and that she got with this person against her better judgment.

Over time, we restarted our relationship, but things were never the same. She had no interest in reconnecting emotionally with me, but I was willing to take her back. The only part of me that was happy about the arrangement was the codependent part that couldn't just let her go.

During a meeting with my boss, I began to confide in her on a personal level. "I would like to leave LA, but I would like to stay with Kaiser. I need a change in my life and work."

She nodded her head. "Well there's actually a job opening up at a new hospital in Oregon."

A glimmer of hope! "Where in Oregon?"

"It's in a city called Hillsboro. It's a suburb about forty miles from Portland."

I joked, "Hillsboro? It doesn't sound like a place where a gay Black woman can thrive."

She brushed it off. "Well, there's a manager position, which is something up there that you could apply to. There's a high likelihood that it's the right job for you, if you want it."

In my head I was thinking, *Oh god, I need to get back into leadership, make a little more money, and do things that really serve me. This might be the right opportunity at the right time.* This was a brand-new hospital and one where I'd be considered one of its founders, which sounded very exciting to me. Many of these hospitals have been around for fifty to sixty years, so being able to get in on the ground floor was something that greatly appealed to me, and I thought it would be a significant career boost as well.

Immediately after that talk with my boss, I asked her to put in a recommendation for me, and I flew out to Portland soon after. Dionne accompanied me and was there to help me look for housing as well. The codependent part of me started to imagine what it would be like for the two of us if we moved out here, what deals we could get on a two-bedroom apartment. I looked at everything and wondered whether she'd be happy out here, never even asking myself whether I was going to be happy there.

After flying into Portland, I soon realized during that thirty-minute drive to Hillsboro that we were no longer in a big city but in more of a small-town vibe. The most significant difference was the massive corporate buildings they were starting to create in the area. Along with the Kaiser building, there were multiple Intel buildings, but it was a nice and up-and-coming area.

Walking into the hospital for the first time was breathtaking. I'd never walked into a hospital system, facility, or clinic that was so new and vibrant. Engineers created it from renewed substances and materials. Walking through the entryway was like walking into a five-star resort, with glass doors surrounded by glass walls, and a beautiful chandelier hung down from the ceiling. The walls inside were lined with art from local, native, Black and Indigenous artists from the area. It was like a dream to walk through.

The job interview once again felt more like a CIA interrogation than an interview. We moved to the basement office of the volunteer services department, and I sat in front of a panel of hospital directors and executives. I learned that in addition to being a manager of a program overseeing hospital volunteers and interns, the position would be managed by the director of nursing, for some reason. Equally shocking was that I would have to build a presence in the hospital gift shop. Inside, I couldn't believe it. *Are you kidding me?*

A gift shop? I don't even enjoy shopping at a grocery store, and now I'd be responsible for an entire store? The more I thought about it, the more I warmed to the idea, because how often in my life would I have a chance to see something built from the ground up?

The panel started to scrutinize every detail of my resume. It was like being interviewed by the senate committee; they asked me about everything from the work that I'd done for Kaiser and my work experience in Phoenix to my personal background. Nothing was left unquestioned, and they left no stone unturned.

The chief nursing officer asked, "You seem to have a short timeline of positions you worked in."

I started to defend my position. "Well I owned a business. I owned a business for six or seven years at that time."

"But this isn't a business, this is a hospital," she rebutted. "You have hospital experience, but it's all been in learning and development. What makes you think you could run this?"

I took a breath and proceeded to dive into my qualifications like a true boss. I made sure this panel knew I meant business and that my experiences could be very useful for the success of this hospital, especially in the gift shop. My mind was racing and working every angle to reassure them that I was the right person. But was I?

The panel seemed impressed, but I couldn't help feel like they were sizing me up as I'd experienced throughout my career. Was I too young? Was I too business-like? Did I even know what I was talking about? As anticipation ran through my body, I realized I'd done everything I could to sell myself, and now it was in their hands.

Upon leaving the interview room, I took a deep breath, feeling like I had just left a battlefield. I told Dionne afterward that I wasn't sure they liked me at all due to the grilling I took from the panel. I assumed it was a wasted trip, so we prepared for our return to LA.

A bit later, we went across the street to grab lunch, and after my first bite of salad I got a call from the director of nursing.

"Hi Kelli, thank you for coming in. I'm so sorry if we were a little hard on you today. We all really did like you."

"No, no of course not!" I was lying of course.

"Okay, well we really enjoyed meeting you, and we'll be in touch."

"Okay." I hung up the phone and turned to Dionne.

"They're not going to call me back."

"Well, why would she call you if they aren't going to call you back?"

"I don't know. Maybe she's just nice?" I shrugged. In my mind, I was starting to see myself living here, but I didn't want to put too much thought into it. Not until I got something concrete.

We got back to LA a few days later, and within a week I got the call offering me the job. I couldn't believe it. I was in shock given the inquisition I'd received from the group. I was relieved, but suddenly I realized that would mean moving to a new town where I knew absolutely no one. They wanted me to start right away, but first I had to go through the rigmarole of background checks and paperwork. And with the holidays right around the corner, they said they'd start the process in January and I'd be expected to start in March. "Do you accept?"

"Yes, yes of course! Thank you so much."

I was over the moon, but it was quickly eclipsed by the idea of starting in March. *March?* I had to figure out how to upend life in only a few months.

News of this new opportunity was the final straw on the camel's back that led to the end of my life with Dionne. She wasn't going to move up to this small town she had no connection in. In the end, it made sense; our lives were going down two different pathways, and I couldn't hold onto her anymore. It was the forced separation I needed. Even if I couldn't commit to separating myself from her by my own hands, I was grateful this came along when I needed it the most.

Getting the call that I had the job was incredible to hear, but knowing I had to pack up my life and relocate in only a few months was daunting. I'd not only have to find a new place to live in an area I had been to only once before but figure out what bare essentials I could bring. Dionne and I worked it out that she would keep hold of the house and help sell my car when I was gone. Pretty quickly, each day became consumed with either work or the move. But each was a day closer to when I could start fresh, literally.

❧ ❧ ❧

In January, I flew out to Oregon and met up with a local friend who agreed to help me look for an apartment. As it turned out, an apartment complex across the street from the hospital was offering a special discount for Kaiser new hires who were moving to the area and seeking housing. It was a perfect deal that I felt was meant to be, so I jumped on it.

With everything set and ready to go, I packed up the few things I had with me—a couch, lawn chairs, clothes, and my cat, Suzy—loaded them all into a big Penske moving truck, then traveled up the coast. With only four days until my actual start date, I didn't have time to do much other than focus on the road in front of me.

There wasn't enough time to do any sightseeing, but I looked back at California in the side mirrors with a sigh. There had been some career and monumental highs since my move to LA. Starting a new career and following where this new road took me. I have been truly blessed, from receiving my master's degree to launching innovative programs for a major health system. Los Angeles was also a place that held the lowest points of my life. Regardless, all of the experiences I'd gone through had led me to this point now. Good and bad, they are and always will be a part of me. Now all I could do was keep driving toward the future I wanted to create for myself.

❧ ❧ ❧

The total trip to Hillsboro was only three days, thank god, but that was cutting it close. There wasn't any time to waste, and unfortunately I was forced to keep the Penske as my big yellow mode of transportation for at least a month after arriving. Not everything starts off on the right foot.

I got the keys from the front desk and found my apartment quickly. I started to unload Suzy and her cat litter first, but just as I entered the front door I tripped and all the cat litter exploded onto the floor. Welcome home, Kelli!

Thankfully, I wasn't alone in unpacking a truck's worth of things.

Around midnight, I had a chance to lie down, set an alarm, and take a breath. The move was complete. I'd officially moved on. Tomorrow was the start of something new.

Chapter 11

Peace

Foundations, Spring 2013

Heading into work the next morning felt invigorating and different from other first days. Walking into the building, everything still had a bright and shiny look to it, a sparkle to every corner and the paint still drying. To help kickstart the hospital, Kaiser had spent millions on marketing campaigns in Oregon to recruit locals to join the foundational team, and as I walked in, so did roughly fifty other new hires. It was a new experience for all of us.

From day one, all of us hit the ground running. There were plenty of us to help fill new roles, but we'd need a lot more filled to get things running like other hospitals, and we also needed to establish all our policies and procedures. Being a part of the managerial staff also meant that I was a part of all the leadership meetings with the C-suite, setting the tone for years to come.

Long hours and little sleep came with the description, but the perks came from knowing I was capable of building something from the ground up. For the first time in my career, I was one of many founders of one the largest hospital systems in the state. I was there to create foundational steps in this hospital that would help build one of the most innovative systems in the Pacific Northwest. I was part of making history. I was part of the founding leadership team and the branding before we even opened the hospital. Every day, I could see the development in real time. Blood, sweat, and tears were put into every corner of this hospital.

The biggest accomplishments of my career came from this work, and it helped me carve a path for the future. I was able to build an internship program and a boutique gift shop from scratch. Thankfully, I had the privilege of being supported by some of the best volunteers in the world. I spent countless hours building something great with very little to work with, learning how to budget on a larger scale and manage the amount of money that was allocated to me and my department. Six months after we opened in August, sixty people were on the volunteer roster, and by the time I left the program we had over a hundred and fifty people registered as volunteers. It was quite an achievement that I continue to be proud of today.

As the internship program began to grow, we focused on identifying students who showed interest in becoming doctors and nurses, but we wanted to give young people an opportunity to work alongside a clinician and witness the day-to-day practice of their field of interest. This was a unique way for students to gain on-the-job training in a state-of-the-art hospital. I worked on the program details with the nurses and physicians in the building and paired students with them. Teaching and mentoring were always emphasized in the advocacy of patient health, so each week my team and I presented at local high schools, colleges, and other recruitment events to showcase the program, and we spent hours talking to any young person who'd listen about the wonderful world of the medical field. As a non-clinician, I was fascinated to find how much knowledge of the field had been ingrained into my brain from my many years of working at Kaiser.

It was important for me to create an atmosphere of learning for those who joined our programs, but I also believed it must be fun. Our volunteers consisted of not only students but older adults who were excited to deliver mail, run the coffee cart, and sell some rather interesting jewelry. What became an integral part of this program was allowing these volunteers the opportunity to train with the hospice community, a practice that helps people transition from life and gives them a peaceful passing. At the time, the idea of student interns participating in a hospice program at this magnitude was unique to our hospital system. It became one of the most popular volunteer opportunities, and many of those who participated became hospice nurses later in life. The focus of the program was to create opportunities to experience what it really feels like to be part of a hospital, so I made sure that if they wanted to, they could be a part of and see every aspect of a hospital system. Many of the student volunteers have gone on to become clinicians.

Putting my thoughts and ideas into action created programs that offered opportunities for people to work together regardless of their race, ethnicity, sexual orientation, or gender identity. The gift shop volunteers included an incredible group of retirees, including some veterans who wanted to make a difference in the lives of the people who walked through the doors. They inspired me to never give up and to see the bright side of impossible situations. The internship program further diversified as students from various ranges of identities applied. I wanted to include everyone, especially people who may have been underrepresented in healthcare. It became my mission to ensure that everyone received a chance to learn and to be a part of something greater than themselves.

For the next two years, I worked six days a week, sometimes twelve- to fifteen-hour days, with no assistant but with a trusty group of volunteers who walked with me every step of the way to make this dream a reality. I was entrenched in all parts of the job, but I loved every second of it. It felt like I was meant to do this work. Every day, I woke up with the thought of how I was going to improve at what I was doing. How was I going to better myself to better help serve society?

For the first time in a decade, I finally felt I could focus on what I wanted. I took more stock in KELLI, in what I wanted to achieve and what I wanted to do for myself every day. I began to make friends, take long road trips, and experience life as a single woman with nothing to lose, going to concerts alone and watching women's soccer like a proper lesbian. I felt rejuvenated physically, emotionally, and spiritually. I started biking, playing volleyball with a team in the area. Everything felt like I was finally taking control over my own life.

When I was married I lived my life for Dionne; the emphasis was on *her* dreams, *her* ambitions, and *her* interests. Now without her I learned I could do all these things alone and find peace and happiness. I didn't need to always have someone there with me to approve of the activities I knew I enjoyed. Being completely independent really allowed me to rediscover what it meant to find joy in the small things in life. Being alone in a state I had almost no ties to let me rediscover what it meant to be Kelli Houston. Some days I'm still figuring out who she is, but every day I get a better understanding.

Childhood Dreams, Fall 2015

Even after I had spent two years working with Kaiser, thoughts of being a lawyer never left my mind. I still had that childhood dream in me, and the more I worked, the more I couldn't keep the idea out of my head.

The work I was doing was fulfilling and gave me the confidence in myself to create things I never thought possible. But with each day that passed by, my ambitious nature led me to want to do something new. Something different. There was a pull for me to go on to something else, like it knew this wasn't where I was meant to be for the rest of my career and my life. I started looking into the LSAT, the national law exam that allows or denies entry into law school. It was during this period that I had garnered enough confidence to pursue this unbelievable dream, so I decided to leave Kaiser with hope and a promise to myself. I let my staff and boss know what my plans were for the future, and they all supported me. Anxiously, I put in my one-month notice. They were shocked, but they could understand and relate to trying to achieve childhood dreams of being the person we envisioned when we were asked what we wanted to be when we grew up.

I started to study day in and day out, preparing for this exam. I carried with me a level of confidence that I could do anything. I had already climbed this massive mountain, doing things I never thought I could ever do. I created programs and systems I never could've imagined existing, and now there was nothing I couldn't accomplish! By this time, I had seriously started dating again and was living with a woman who encouraged me to do this. According to her, we could make this a reality; this dream could become real. After weeks of studying, as well as sacrificing the financial security and founder position with Kaiser, I . . . didn't perform. I didn't fail the test, but my results weren't enough to get into Harvard Law. Still, I didn't want to just give up because of a not-great test result, so I applied and was accepted into a smaller, online law school.

For the next year, studying and inundating myself in every class became my nine-to-five. It was a grind, and it forced me into a different mindset than when I went for my college degrees. What I hadn't anticipated was the workload. I knew people in law school and attorneys, so I should've known how intensive it was going to be, but you never really know until you're struggling to breathe underneath the coursework and the pressure. The deeper I got into it, the more my confidence lessened. The mental confidence of "I can do this!" when I first started slowly became, "What am I doing here?" I became lazy and unfocused, and with every day that passed I worried more about the finances of this endeavor. The price of law school was $150,000, which was always in the back of my mind. Not having a sense of security created a problem. I thrive when I feel secure both inside and outside, and at this point I was starting to feel like I had neither. I was putting all this effort into something I wanted to chase after all my life, and all I had to show for it right then and there was feeling like a failure.

I couldn't get into the same headspace as my colleagues. My professors saw that and graded me accordingly. I knew legal concepts well enough, but I didn't know how to apply them. That's what law school is: how well you know the history of how the law was applied in previous cases and applying those precedents to real situations and new cases. At my age, I couldn't wrap my head around these concepts the way a more youthful, more recent college graduate could. I hadn't been in college since 2010, and I had to remember all the habits of how I succeeded back then.

Unfortunately, it's about more than just how much you can pull yourself up by your bootstraps. It's also about who's there in your corner cheering you on and encouraging you to keep going when you're at your lowest. When I went through grad school, I had the level of support from friends and from Dionne to help me navigate through those murky waters, but in law school I didn't have that. The person I was dating at the time seem quite ignorant of my goals. When we hung out with her friends, they didn't know what it was like to be put into this type of a grind nor how to support me. I was trapped in a vortex, circling the drain.

I fell into a depression thinking about taking on this seemingly impossible task and realizing I'd have to do this every day. I had made this massive commitment and left my founding position for this. I didn't know how to get out of the quicksand that felt like it was swallowing me whole, bit by bit, day by day. Waking up, I'd put my feet to the ground only to regress to feeling like a failure every day. And every day I felt more alone.

After a year, I couldn't keep churning the same wheel and getting the same result. Something needed to change. I needed to go back to work, and I had to ask myself, *What do I really want to do? If not this, then what?* I wanted to go back into business and civil rights, to blend those fields together in some way, but I just didn't know how to start doing that. Like a wish being granted, someone reached out to me based on the DEI work I had accomplished while at Kaiser. I was a trainer and an educator there for a long time, and this person was looking to expand their diversity initiatives at a local Catholic hospital.

Diversity at a Catholic hospital carried an interesting tone to it, but it was work. And at this point I was willing to jump into anything that would save me from trying to interpret hundred-year-old cases into today's standards.

More than Just a Gig, Fall 2016

Being called in for an interview, I didn't know what to expect, especially coming from a Catholic hospital. They didn't have a job description for me in diversity written out in fine print, but it felt like a great opportunity to dive into something more than having my head stuck between law books.

During the interview process, I was able to meet the executive vice president, who was the one who felt the hospital seriously needed to broaden their thinking and bring healthcare into the twenty-first century. I was intrigued and definitely interested. Although I'm not Catholic, I spent a good amount of my formative years in the church and understood the bigotry that often exists in these institutional settings. This offer also came at a time when Pope Francis made disparaging comments about the LGBTQ+ community, which set off a firestorm of anger and bewilderment within the community I loved so much. The idea that someone in the C-suite wanted to bring diversity initiatives into a Catholic-based hospital was pushing boundaries.

The full details of the consultation were still being formed when I walked into the office to meet for the first time. I looked around the office, which was adorned with civil rights memorabilia, family pictures, and a large print of the hospital's values: Respect, Stewardship, Collaboration, and Social Justice. Aside from those values, the leadership team made a commitment that year to educate their leadership on using such words as stepping stones toward diversity and equity. While I was impressed by this sentiment, I was also confused.

Why now? What changed for them? I knew I wanted to be part of this, but what was it?

My future boss began to speak in more depth about the need for statewide leadership training on becoming stewards of this work. While she spoke, I listened and took notes both mentally and physically. This was the challenge I had been looking for in my career. Goodbye law school, hello Catholic hospital.

She turned to me and said, "We are anxious for you to get started. You set the terms and conditions for doing this work. What is your base commission?"

I froze. It had been years since I put together a consulting agreement for which money was really involved. I had no clue what to charge nor what I was worth. At that very moment, I didn't know what I was worth, but I knew it was a lot! As a Black, gay woman, my insecurities arose from years of internal voices telling me not to do too much, out of fear of losing the job.

Later that evening, I sought my ancestors for advice. I quietly asked my beloved grandmother, who was the best angel I knew at that time, "Grandma, what am I worth?" The next day, she responded. I spent two days writing out a comprehensive contract that included everything except purchasing a jet for me to fly in between meetings. Seriously, I realized that this was my opportunity to stand in my power and take notice of my abilities even if others could not. The more I wrote, the more I recognized that my credentials were just as important as anyone else's, even though this was my first diversity consulting gig.

I wrote out the contract, the details of the work, and made sure I'd be getting paid at the highest rate possible for someone in this emerging field. My soon-to-be boss took it and made no changes to what I proposed. The contract was signed in September 2016, and I was on my way to building a career I never imagined.

Day in and day out, I started to create training modules and materials for the leaders across the hospital system. It would be an introduction to educating them on marginalized people's needs in a hospital setting, and the better part of the year was spent conducting widespread training and education to leadership. After over one thousand leaders had participated in this program with me as their singular educator, the hospital C-suite took notice and proposed an extended plan to further align with the social justice practice of diversity within their health system. It wasn't without complications, as my training sessions were sometimes met with opposition and discord from those who participated. I can remember a time when I was commissioned to conduct two sessions in Ketchikan, Alaska, which had a population of fourteen thousand and only eight hundred medical workers within our hospital. It was a feisty town full of clinicians who didn't understand why we needed this education. I felt as though I needed to write "We are very diverse" on billboards given how much I heard that statement. I cringed each time I stepped into these sessions and saw that more than half the leaders identified as White. So much for diversity. But that was the exact reason I was there to provide education.

It wasn't all doom and gloom. There were light moments as well, such as when a resident employee offered to take a few of us for a drive around the city, which was beautiful. I enjoyed the majesty of the lush green landscape and wildlife that surround the land. I did have moments of stress during this drive because the group wanted to stop at a creek and watch a family of black bears walk along the path. I smiled, yet inside I was reminded of a story I'd heard not too long prior to my visit about a young man in Alaska who had a rather unfortunate experience with a family of bears on a path. I said nothing at first, but as we approached the site and then parked, I observed a father and young son get out of their car and slowly walk to within a few feet away of the path where the bears were. I couldn't take my eyes off them. The young boy couldn't have been more than three or four. At that moment, I whispered to myself in horror, "That's the last time we'll see those two!"

When the time came for us to leave the car, I politely said I could take pictures from my seat, perfectly positioned as far to the back of the SUV as possible. I was not going to tempt fate like that father had with his son. I wanted to live. I'd see too many horror movies to step out of that car with them. I just got this job. I wasn't going to lose my life over it.

To add more to the fun, my traveling colleagues somehow got a memo that I didn't, which was to stay at a place called the Comstock Hotel (not the real name). As a consultant, I was often responsible for my own travel accommodations, but this was a place I wish had been booked for me. At dinner that evening, my colleagues were remarking about how fabulous the hotel was, and I listened without chiming in until they mentioned their luxurious bathroom. My eyes shot over to the large key I'd been given upon check-in at my hotel, which was like the one in *The Shining*. The key was the size given during the Gold Rush, and my room was small, with very little light and only two outlets, two of which were occupying the phone, television, and clock. It was an electrical fire waiting to happen. After the long trip, I decided to check out the restroom, which from my perspective was the smallest bathroom in the entire city and would've been perfect if I were three feet tall. The measurements were completely off, as the shower took up most of the bathroom and left little room for someone to relieve themselves. It was a sight. They also had the gall to put a rotary phone in there for good measure. It was the most uncomfortable place I'd ever been. This was the perfect start to an already testy time, but thankfully it was only for two days. I still couldn't help but envy my traveling colleagues, and I had dreams of being able to use their bathroom just so I could see how the other half lived, but I didn't dare ask.

But I digress. These days in Ketchikan changed my perspective on what matters most about the work I've come to know as my life's work. It was asking the question to those who didn't understand nor care, "Why is diversity work so important?" As I began this career path, I realized that what folks were afraid of was the perspective of looking from within and recognizing that things haven't changed much since the civil rights movement, and it became all too real once Donald Trump was elected president of a widely diverse country.

In 2017, I stepped into a whole new world of reckoning with the fact that as much as the world had changed, our country was still uncertain of how to approach topics such as diversity, inclusivity, and antiracism. These were words that have since become catchphrases, but at that time and before George Floyd, I sensed that White America was not really ready for this work. The more I sensed this ambiguity, the more I stepped into it with vigor and at times anger. There had been deaths at the hands of police, brutal beatings of men of color, and disappearances of Native American women across the country. Additionally, my LGBTQ+ community was equally disappearing into death- and hate-filled rhetoric that continues today. Who was going to stop the madness? I didn't want to be a hero, just to save the lives of people I loved and who loved me. This was the time to step out of the shadows of my insecurity and take the baton of true social justice. Pope Francis was wrong. The LGBTQ+ community, especially the transgender community, *do* deserve the same benefits and health rights as any other human on this planet.

They are my brothers and sisters, and I knew I had to do everything in my power to give them a voice.

It was during this time that the hospital decided it was ready to create more around diversity. My socially conscious supervisor became my heroine in that she stood up for me as the first-ever diversity leader in a Catholic health system, leading efforts to understand how to address healthcare through the lens of equity. I had been with the hospital for only a year, but I knew I was up for the challenge. In May 2017, I was given the opportunity to write my own job description as System Diversity Director. It was an honor that someone had that much faith in my abilities, and I didn't want to screw this up. It was the first step on a new yellow brick road that led me on a path unlike any I've ever known. I was finally moving on up!

Running on Empty

As I started creating unconscious bias training and respectful communication training on behalf of LGBTQ+ patients and families, my work led to ensuring this hospital system made it possible for physicians and surgeons to provide gender affirming care for transgender patients. Major transition-related surgery wasn't on the radar of any Catholic hospitals until 2016.

It was enlightening to see updates to policies and education on how to truly support the community that means so much to me. I could feel how engaged the medical community was with all the implementations I suggested, particularly when it came to supporting leadership in building a more culturally responsive care model. I sensed that folks in my field wanted to be better, to do better for a community that has been misunderstood for decades. They wanted to treat people well, and they were always open to anything I proposed and all the training I prepared. It was a great year and a great feeling to be able to provide this service to our patients, to know that my work was having an immediate impact not just on the staff but also on the patients. We were able to see the positive changes reflected in their experiences, and it felt like everything was coming together. I was watching this beautiful house start to take shape after having started from nothing but a plot of land.

The deeper I dove into this with my team, the more I realized this was the work I was meant to be doing. Being able to create these programs, these changes, and see the real benefit for the people I was serving gave me a deep sense of purpose and belonging. I wasn't just creating a training module or helping someone understand what it means to use someone's correct pronouns. I could see the positive impact on my community, and that gave me all the pride in the world.

Unfortunately, the higher ups started to get wind of the changes that were being put in place, and they weren't the happiest about all the new initiatives and policies. The good work I was doing only became more difficult when my boss retired. Upon her departure, it became clear that diversity wasn't on the menu for them as a long-standing practice. I started to feel a sense of dread that they weren't eager to keep me on the payroll. To this institution, diversity was considered just an HR policy initiative, relegated to behind-the-scenes paperwork that didn't serve the communities at large. My focus was always on the hospital and creating best practices to develop a more equitable landscape for all our patients, to ensure that everyone received the same level of care. My boss was replaced with someone who didn't share same vision for this work. She sought to relegate this work only to training. We butted heads constantly about this, each of us trying to pull it in one direction, but in the end I knew this was a war I could not win. Without the support of my boss, the programs and training I wanted to include would never be approved.

Leaving the position was not an ideal situation, but I had carved this niche for myself as a trainer, an educator, and someone able to build these systems and training programs for a health system from scratch. I could take this anywhere because there were now diversity positions everywhere. People were starting to understand the need to hire experts in this field to talk about racial justice and inequalities in hospital systems. The number of Black patients who weren't receiving the same level of care as their White counterparts was increasing, and people were finally starting to take notice.

In my research, I came across a children's hospital that had just been named one of the top ten children's hospitals in the country. They were seeking a new director for the Center of Health Equity and Diversity. I felt like I might be in over my head, like this was the highest of ambitions, but I set my sights high, sent in my application, and thought, *Well, if it happens, it happens.* I couldn't believe they wanted to interview me given my time in the field, but I made the hour and a half journey with all the confidence I could muster.

During the initial interview, I was filled with trepidation about whether I could do this job. They scrutinized the fact that I'd fully been in the role for only the past two years, as well as the fact that this position had a lot of turnover. I would be the center's third director in the last four years, and they were not anxious to hire and lose another director and have to search for a fourth. When I brought up that I'd been in hospital systems since 2008, they questioned my having had multiple jobs in the past decade. I started to feel really small in this meeting, and when it ended I left with the same sinking feeling I had when I interviewed with Kaiser in Hillsboro. I knew I wasn't at my best, and I felt like cold, gray rain as I drove back. I was despondent about the whole experience, and coming home didn't help. I was quietly fighting with my partner at the time.

At this point I was so career-driven I didn't care about relationships. I didn't want to go through the same song and dance of convincing others of my worth and determining whether we were actually compatible. I was in my late forties, and I was seeing the real impact my work was having on people's lives. That's where my heart was. I am a Black, woman, and I am able to help people in my community. Doing this work became about more than the work itself. The work I was doing transcended me; it was about helping everyone I could and making a real difference in this world, one that has consistently put me and my communities down for our identities. I wanted to put all my focus and energy into this work, and I was despondent to think that there was practically no chance I'd get the job.

What didn't help the situation was that I was suddenly in the throes of perimenopause. I began to experience feelings of frustration and anger at the pull of a hair trigger. What we don't tell women in their forties is that they're not going crazy, their bodies are changing. That's a big reason for depression and could also explain the challenges I was experiencing in my personal relationships. I also didn't have a partner who could relate to my struggles, which created more complications in my life. After two months, I still couldn't find a doctor who could give me the whole picture, but I was a lesbian on birth control. That was the recourse I was forced into due to the lack of experience from my physician.

In the midst of this turmoil, I received an email from the children's hospital with some good news. I'd almost forgotten I was interviewing for the job given the lengthy time it took to hear back. I was informed that I would be interviewing with the chief HR officer who would be overseeing the role. I went in, met them for lunch, and a few weeks later they offered me the job. I was stunned. I mean, the fact that they brought me back for a second interview after two months meant they were definitely interested, yet I still felt a sense of imposter syndrome. Still, I wasn't going to turn down this opportunity to lead an entire center focused on health equity. Their offer came with the caveat that I move closer for this job, and my perimenopausal brain instantly said, "Fuck this place. I'm moving." I didn't have the support network I needed here anymore, and I needed a change of pace. I tried to make it work with my partner in a long-term relationship, but like most unstable relationships, things fizzled out.

I never expected that taking this job would change the way I viewed health equity. We were in the middle of the first Trump administration, and the mass deportations he was orchestrating had a serious impact on the work I was doing. One of the most unexpected parts of my job came in 2018 when our center was working to ensure that children who visited our hospital were provided with a safe space while in our care. This was also the time when Immigration and Customs Enforcement officers were navigating through hospitals across the country with threats of separating families, especially those who were identified as undocumented. At the center, we were collaborating with providers and the legal department to ensure we alleviated any fears that children would be transported illegally from our hospital. Immigrant mothers who were pregnant were neglecting their prenatal plans and care out of fear that a nurse or doctor would call enforcement to have them taken away, and there had been suspicion that clinical teams across the country were taking it upon themselves to report innocent children and their families.

The Trump Administration was adamant about rounding up whomever they deemed as "undocumented," and there were plenty of bad agents who were more than willing to blow the proverbial whistle on anyone who "looked like an immigrant."

With the support of my boss and the legal department, I, along with the chief medical officer, was permitted to send out a memo to all leaders in the hospital announcing that my team would make strides to protect all patients: "We will treat anyone who sets foot in this hospital, and they are under our protection." I set up patient navigators to meet with patients based on their identities, and they met and worked directly with the patients and helped put their minds at ease when discussing the care they needed. These patient navigators were people of color, Somalian, LGBTQ+, Hispanic, Asian, and even Russian. We also worked with tribal counties to make sure they were being treated daily and that they had access to the hospital. I made sure that no matter who someone was, no matter their identity, each had someone who knew their experiences and could be there to support them and their family throughout our system.

While setting up these systems and continuing to develop training, I heard a code call in a unit that signaled a concern with one of the patients. While these codes are important to denote an emergency in a unit or facility, there were times these calls were deemed inequitable and my team would have to step in to investigate. In one unfortunate case, a call for restraint was put in place to request security's assistance in managing a three-year-old Black child who was experiencing difficulty with taking an IV. What I never expected to see and still shakes me to this day was learning that this call resulted in this child being detained and held down with force by the security team until he calmed down.

I lost it. This felt like something that couldn't be real. He was three years old and having an outburst, and that did not (and never does) call for violent force being thrust upon him to make him stop. I could not believe what I was seeing. My first thought was, *How do we eliminate this code and ensure there is psychological safety in this system?* Seeing this completely changed my focus on what it meant to be a person of color and what it meant to be one in a hospital system.

In conjunction with the chief medical officer, my team responded by creating a policy that would permeate across our organization: If anyone engaged in any behavior even remotely within a millimeter close to what was done to this child, they risked being fired and having legal action taken against them. There was zero tolerance for this. Under no circumstances should anyone, especially in a hospital, fear the threat of violence for any reason, let alone have that happen to them. A hospital is a place where people come for treatment, not from where emotional scars are made. Since that moment, I have strived to do more to ensure that no child ever feels the way that child felt and that no parent or child feared being taken away and thrown into a country that was unfamiliar to them simply because of their skin color or status. This hospital was a place for everyone.

During my time there, I wrote a three-year strategic plan that included gender clinics for anyone in the LGBTQ+ community who needed care. I developed LGBTQ+ models for nursing and providers, and I carved out an understanding with all our nurses about the importance of addressing trans care and what that looked like, not only for adults but for young transgender children, where it's crucial. We worked to address systemic racism in hospital systems, and we trained nurses and doctors about how policies and treatment of people of color have been pervasively leading to the erosion of trust in the medical field. We listened to their needs and concerns and focused on how we could earn the trust of those who'd been constantly overlooked and overshadowed. This work became about trying to help course correct a system that has favored one particular type of person in this industry and create an equitable and sustainable practice that served everyone who stepped through the doors. It may have taken decades for me to carve the path I needed to find my passion, but I did. Since my first leap into diversity work, I knew I had found a world where I could be my most authentic self, and with every day I do this work, I know that I'm helping someone's life out there. I may not meet them, I may never know their name and they may never know mine, but knowing I've made a difference is all I need to know this is where I was meant to be.

Forgiveness and Reconnection, Summer 2018

It had been years since I made the last call to my parents, yet my dad continued to remain in contact. He would call me every weekend with great attempts to get me to reach out in return, usually telling me in a voicemail to call my mom. I again ignored his calls every time. When he learned how to text, he would send things like "I. Love. You." and I ignored those as well. The stubborn Aries in me was in denial that my family really cared about me, and I continued to ignore them though I longed to reconnect with them.

For about two years, my dad continued to try to make contact with me. It wasn't until a few months after my move to Oregon that I got a text from Kim. We hadn't spoken in two years, but somehow she got my new number, which surprised me. I knew something had to be wrong to hear from anyone in my family, especially now. The text read, "I know we haven't talked in a while, but Dad is having some health issues and we all need to get on a family call."

As I looked down at the text, it felt like the world started to slow down. I wondered what was wrong. *Was Dad sick? Was he in the hospital?* I didn't understand. *Was he injured? Some accident?* So many thoughts were running through my mind. I couldn't catch them all, but I anxiously pondered what was next.

I was still pissed off at my family, but I needed to be there. He was still my dad. I called Kim and she filled me in on the details. He'd been diagnosed with multiple myeloma, for which he had been undergoing treatment for the past ten years and had lost a considerable amount of weight for a man who was generally in good physical shape. It was becoming more serious, and he began to open up to the family about his cancer. My belief is that he tried to keep things hidden from everyone and to tackle this on his own so he didn't worry anyone. He was always a man of pride, and I admire his strength in maintaining that level of pain and suffering for as long as he did.

The more I heard, the more it felt like the blood was rushing out of my body. Hearing that your parent has cancer is a hard pill to swallow.

As soon as I got off the phone with Kim, I called my dad. He acted nonchalant, as if nothing happened, as if he knew this call was going to happen sooner or later.

"Hey, Dad, how are you?"

"I'm okay. Hey, let me put you on with your mom." He was always so insistent to get me to talk with her again.

I cut him off. "No no no, let me talk to you."

A brief moment of silence.

"Kim talked to me about your treatments." I didn't want to directly say it was cancer and neither did he. It was almost as if it were a taboo word that would make it all the more real if spoken out loud.

"Yes, I'm getting treatments done, but I don't want to talk about that. How are you doing?!"

"That's a long story, Dad, but I'm doing good. I started a new job and now live in Oregon. I'm very happy, but I'm concerned about you and Mom."

"That's great! It's good to hear you're doing well. Are you coming home?"

"Thanks, Dad, and yes I'm planning a trip now." It felt good to hear him happy for me.

"That's good because your mom wants to see you," he asserted, always focused on everyone else.

"How about you?" I asked. "Do *you* want to see me?"

With a chuckle, he said, "I guess! Well, let us know when you're coming in, and we'll pick you up from the airport."

"Okay. I'm going to let you go. I've got to get back to work. I'll call you and Mom back in a few days."

"Sounds good. We'll talk soon."

Just as I was about to hang up the phone, he added, "Oh wait! I love you, Kelli."

Hearing him say that shook me. He never said that first; it was always a response to a family member saying it to him.

"I love you too, Dad. I'll see you soon."

I left that call with a lingering feeling after having heard him say that. I knew it came from his heart. It wasn't like the typical call and the responses of "Hey, how are you?/Good, how are you?" Hearing him say that reaffirmed to me that no matter what, my dad loved me. No matter who I am or what I do, he will always love me.

From that day forward, I made sure to always say I love you. I said it every time I saw him, every time I called him, and every time

I texted him. I'm grateful I had the wisdom to say it that many times and to hear him say it back.

❧ ❧ ❧

Immediately upon getting off the plane in Reno, every moment felt tense. Every part of me was steaming with anxiety, unsure what my parents would say after not seeing me for so long, especially since I brought my girlfriend at the time, Stephanie. I was grateful to have her there with me, and I wanted to be my full self around my parents.

I kept in my heart the "I love you" my dad said to me, and for the most part everything seemed normal. Well, as normal as can be when you see your parents again after so long. Being on guard the whole time, I was expecting something to happen, some comment or someone to say something, but no. They were just happy to see me in person. And they accepted Stephanie in a way I never expected a girlfriend of mine to be accepted. My mom liked that she was friendly and was cordial to her the entire time.

We went to lunch at a Mexican restaurant we've been going to as a family since I was six. My parents have known the owners since they opened in 1971, and they always make room for us whenever we come in. It felt good to be back in such a familiar place and to introduce it to Stephanie.

Without missing a beat, my dad, who loves to stir shit up, wanted to put everything out on the table: "So why didn't you talk to us for so long?"

Okay, great. I relax for five minutes, and I forget any responses I planned. "Uhhhhh . . . well . . . that's a, uh, complex question, Dad." I didn't know how to answer that. How do you boil down years of trauma and how you've felt for decades into a few short sentences?

My mom quickly jumped on the fire before it spread: "We're not going to talk about that here."

Bury it and say everything's fine. That was the practice of the family, and it was going to be continued.

We had a nice meal together as a family, continuing on like everything was fine. Both my parents were copacetic, and they never had any visceral reactions to anything I told them. All I knew was that I was hoping they'd both accept that I was finally happy in my life and that I had a partner in Stephanie, which wasn't going to change. I knew I had to be the adult in the room when it came to staying true to myself and what I needed to stay sane. I believed that this time around, my parents were certain that if they didn't accept their daughter for who she was, it would make it difficult for me to continue being part of their lives and more time would be lost. With my dad's cancer diagnosis, I knew in my heart that this was my opportunity to be there in a time of crisis like never before. I had no intention of running away because I never wanted to live in regret if my dad passed.

❧ ❧ ❧

For the next five years, I went home religiously and slowly began reconnecting with both my parents. We were able to rebuild our relationship and start to repair the damage that was done. My mom never really apologized for what happened, but I knew she loved me. My dad and I made amends with each other, and he was the one who fully accepted me. He was reborn from his illness, and I think he knew he didn't have a lot of time left. Although he never let on to this fact, I could sense it by the way he found time for me and wanted to share with me, even when it was simply sitting together and watching a round of golf. He wanted to live every day as it came, and he appreciated any time he was able to have with me.

The more time I spent with my parents, the more I started to forgive them and wanted to be there for both of them. It took years of therapy to work past my internalized anger about what happened and accept where we all were now. It was by no means an easy thing to work through. Yet isn't that the truth for just about all queer people working through their relationships with their parents? Above all, though, I was grateful to have my parents back in my life. I cherish the time we were able to have together, the moments when we sat down on the couch and just talked or enjoyed the time being around each other, reconnecting as father and daughter. He began asking me about my career and consistently asked, "What is that you do again?" He seemed relieved that I was finally home and could be with the family. It was like he was at peace with the thought that his family was back together again, that we were catching up on all the small details between us, all we'd missed out on from each other's lives when we didn't see each other. It was the first time in a long time I felt that special connection between parent and child.

I flew in frequently to spend time with my dad, and I was there with him when he went to his doctor appointments. Every time, I'd sit there anxiously hoping to hear some good news about how his condition was improving or that the treatments were working well for him. But every time I could see him slowing down. Still, he insisted on doing things on his own and still wanted to have that level of independence he'd had for a majority of his life, such as driving to his own doctor's appointments and making sure he could walk on his own. He wanted to ensure his life was his own, no matter what.

There were some fun moments, such as when my dad was still recovering from a ruptured spleen and stopped eating anything but ice cream. His eyesight had started to go bad, but he still wanted to go to Wendy's to get a burger and ice cream. So when he told us all that he was going out on his own, there was no stopping him. My brother and I were home at the time, and when he hadn't come back after thirty minutes, Mom said, "Someone needs to go find your dad."

Naturally it was up to the kids to find him, but we had to devise a plan to retrace his steps. We found the nearest Wendy's and started to look around to see whether we could find his car anywhere nearby. Lo and behold, we saw him crawling across the street, going at his own speed and making sure he was the absolute safest he could possibly be on the road. It was a relief to see him, and my brother suggested we should follow him home from a few car-lengths behind. We made sure to keep our distance as if we were protecting the president from any possible harm. Other cars would honk and speed around him, but nothing stopped him from going his own speed. He made it home safely, and he was none the wiser to us trailing him back.

My dad needed things to be as normal as possible. If we ever went out anywhere, he needed to be the one driving. He thought we drove too fast, while he drove two miles an hour, crawling to a stop sign in the neighborhood and then slamming on the brakes when we finally got to the stop sign.

There was a time when we got a call from our family friend who was a ninety-year-old woman needing my dad to help her start her car at 8:00 p.m. My dad was eighty-one at the time and couldn't see well, especially at night, and he had just had a blood transfusion that day, but promptly made his way to the door. I called out to him, "Do you want us to go with you?"

"No, it'll be fine. I'm going to follow her home."

"So it's the blind leading the blind home."

It was such a ridiculous situation, but it's what he wanted, and he wasn't going to relinquish control of how he lived his life. He was always there to help people who needed him, he never stopped putting people first, and community always meant a lot to him. During the time we spent together, there were also many milestones we celebrated as a family, including my parents' sixtieth wedding anniversary. My parents wanted to renew their vows, and we hosted a huge party for them. Family friends, relatives, and community members all wanted to make this a huge celebration of their life together that mirrored when they got married six decades prior. People from across the country came in to celebrate with us. Kim and I gave my mom away, my brother was my dad's best man, and our uncle was the pastor. Seeing my parents recreate their vows is a special memory that continues to bring warmth to my heart.

We made sure to celebrate all the big and small moments together. We got together when my niece graduated college, and my dad was recognized for his service as the first Black police officer in Reno and by the Air Force for being one of the first Black coders for the local base. We made sure to all come together and tear up the neighborhood in celebration. There were a lot of milestones that allowed us to reconnect with each other, and I'll always be grateful for every moment I got to spend with my father and the entire family. It would soon be that many of these moments would become few and far between.

❧ ❧ ❧

Throughout his cancer treatments, Dad made it a point to hide his appointments from Mom or refuse to take her with him. I can only speculate that he didn't want her to know how things were progressing and wanted to protect her from the reality of what was happening.

In mid-June of 2018, he broke that rule. The way my mom tells the story, he wanted her to come to his last appointment. They sat in the office waiting for the doctor to hopefully bring some good news. He had the opposite.

The doctor looked at my dad with sorrow written on his face. "The blood transfusions are no longer working. I'm sorry, Mr. Houston. There's no more treatment we can offer you now."

According to my mom, Dad bowed his head and said nothing as they left the office.

Both of them remained silent; there was nothing more that could be said. No amount of protesting or outrage could help at this point, and there was nothing more to say to the doctor. When they climbed into the car with only the wind playing in the background, my mom looked at my dad and saw the moment the light went right out of his eyes. They both knew what was going to happen.

My dad never returned to the hospital and refused to leave his bed for anything. He wanted to be in the comfort of his own home. The only person he allowed to give him morphine injections was my high school friend Jasmine, who had become a nurse and whom he recognized from our years of friendship. He trusted her.

On that fateful day, Jasmine was visiting my parents when she called me to tell what my dad's situation was. "Kelli, you need to come home. Your dad isn't doing well."

My heart rate jumped when I heard those words. I knew this was coming. You see it happen in front of you, but nothing really prepares you for it when you know it's the end.

"Okay, I will get on the horn with Kim and Robert to get them out there too. Please take care of him until I get there."

I scheduled a flight out as soon as I could. The earliest flight was on July 2. I called Dad the day before to let him know I had the flight booked and would see him soon. I asked him how he was feeling and whether the morphine was helping. It wasn't an hour-long call, and at the end he could barely talk, but he whispered, "I love you, Kelli."

"I love you too, Dad." Those were the last words I said to him.

The night before I was supposed to fly out, I couldn't sleep. Something was preventing it from happening, some force was keeping me awake. I lay awake in bed until 3:00 a.m. and I felt him. That's when I realized what was keeping me awake. It was my dad. His energy, his life, was leaving him. He couldn't hold on, and I could feel him passing. It's something I can't describe other than to say I could feel him passing. I held in my heart the words he spoke to me the day before: "I love you, Kelli."

Subconsciously I understand why he said those words. It was as if he knew he wouldn't be able to hold on until I got there. He needed to let me know, no matter what happened, no matter where my life went. All that I was, all that I am, he accepted me unconditionally, and he loved and supported me with all his heart.

I closed my eyes, and with his final words in my heart, I knew he would live with me and be with me forever, watching over me as I continue to walk my own path forward.

Epilogue: A Life for Me

Since writing this memoir, both my parents have passed. It has been difficult at times, yet it's reassuring to know they're both together with my grandparents, aunt, and friends I've lost over the years. They're my angels all looking over me. Each and every day, I know in my heart as they watch over me that they're all proud of the woman I've become.

In the years after my dad's passing, I became grateful to have spent more time with my mom. While we may not have seen eye to eye on everything, we continued to make amends with each other. I continued to visit home regularly, and we worked hard to connect with each other as any mom and daughter would. It was nice to be able to spend time together and enjoy each other's company. Unexpectedly, Mom was struck down by a stroke in July of 2023. Once again, the family reunited to be by her side. As she lay in her hospital bed, hooked up to machines with irreversible brain damage from the stroke, the ICU doctor approached my siblings about her condition, which would leave her unable to function without continuous hospitalization and inability to speak. In a word, she was already gone.

As a sibling group, we made the most difficult decision we ever had to make, and that was to let Mom go in peace. We agreed to remove any additional life support measures, and she would go into hospice the next day. That evening, it was my turn to sleep in the room with her. As I lay on the hard hospital family mattress with the sound of gospel music playing in the background for comfort, my life with my mom flashed before my eyes, and the realization that I would never talk to her, hug her, or even hear her voice again struck me to my core. I began to cry. I looked at her, squeezed her hand, and said, "I forgive you, and I hope you forgive me too." A rush of peace fell before me, and I realized in that moment how much I truly would miss her. She was the only mother I had, and now she was gone, but she would live in my heart forever.

As we prepared our families for the inevitable, we crowded around her hospital bed. Old friends, new acquaintances, and family were there, as well as our family minister and his wife. Those who loved my mom, people whose life she touched, surrounded her and wanted to be there in her final moments. Mom had other plans. During hospice treatment, she continued to hang on, giving more and more family and friends the chance to say goodbye. Finally, on July 18 at 10:00 p.m., my mom peacefully left this world to join the love of her life, and our grandparents. My sister was the only one in the room and witnessed her passing. I rushed to the hospital to give Mom a final kiss goodbye, and when I leaned over I could hear the faint sound of a British accent. It was at that time I realized that one of her favorite audiobooks by Prince Harry was playing in the background. I thought, *Oh God, please don't tell me that my mom passed to the sound of Prince Harry talking about the size of his member.*

In the end, I know that I was deeply loved by my parents and that she and everyone I've lost in my life are up there watching over me. Trust me, I need those angels.

So why did I write this book? It's simple: I am starved for affection. Seriously, in my business and my life, I am on a mission to inspire others to make the impossible possible. It's possible to go back to school and complete your education and advance your career. It's possible to pursue your dreams, and even if they may not be what you thought, they may lead you in the direction you needed to be going in all along. It's possible to come out on the other side of facing your own adversities, conflicts, and struggles along the way and come out stronger from it.

As I've gone through my own stages of life, I've realized it's not always about romantic relationships. I've tried to hold onto romantic relationships my entire life, and if there's one thing they've taught me, it's that I can move through this world without them. I have learned to enjoy my own company without fear that I will die alone. I am not alone. I am happy and at peace.

It's a lesson that has taken several decades to learn, but it's what helped turn me away from one of the most desperate times of my life, one that led to the decision no longer exist, and toward the Kelli I am today, who chooses to embrace life to the fullest. I have been blessed beyond belief, and I have some incredible angels watching over me.

The more my life has changed and evolved, the more I've grown disinterested in trying to please the people who don't matter to me. I try my best to keep around me only the people I know matter. They are the people who are there for me, the ones who offer their shoulder when I need to cry and who share a drink with me when I want to celebrate.

All the stages in my life have helped lead me to this moment now, where I'm able to share this story with you. I've grown from being the terrified child in the closet who was forced back into it. When I was finally out, I was out for good. My life experiences have given me the confidence to stand up for who I am and for those in my community. My mission and my work will always continue to be advocating for those who feel that no one is in their corner.

Throughout my life, people have come and gone, and the cheerleaders are growing more in heaven than down here on Earth. If you're in a similar place, then let these words serve as the confidence booster you need to be who you are. Do it for you and no one else. Because the world needs more of you in it. You can take your life into your own hands and shape yourself into whoever you want to be. No matter what, no one can take away who you are. You can create the life you want for yourself. And I'll always be there in your corner.

Acknowledgments

The book is a love letter to myself and to my LGBTQ+ community, and it would not have been possible without my writing colleague and editor, Brandi Lai, who spent hours upon hours with me over the past five years as I reminisced, sharing very private, personal, and often scary memories. I thank her for her patience, understanding, and insight throughout this journey. Special appreciation to Jen T. Grace, Catherine Whiting and the entire Publish Your Purpose (PYP) family for their support, advocacy and guidance in making my memoir a reality.

I would like to thank my family and loved ones who contributed to this book both directly and indirectly. Without you all, my life would've been quite boring. Thanks to the RHS Class of '89 crew, my dear friends who inspired many beautiful stories in life (Lisa, Jennifer P., and Manny).

To my heavenly angels and cheerleaders Suzy, Angie, Bobby, Rick, my parents, and my maternal and paternal grandparents, who will always hold a special place in my heart.

Special thanks to my sister, Kimberly, brother, Robert Keith, and my beloved niece and nephews Brianna, Jarred (and his wife, Taylor), and Bryce (and his wife, Savannah), whom I love with all my heart. Special special thanks to Miki and Bru for bringing love, laughter and peace back to my life.

Thanks to my professional colleagues across the country. You are all supportive, caring, and educated folks whom I admire and hold with great esteem, especially Pleasant Radford Jr., Rhodes Perry, Shawna Unger, Meredith Anastasio, Sue Orchard, Edwin Lindo Jr., Cheryl Mansfield, Farah Council, Jane Renken, Kim Smith, Heather Boetto, Alan Lederman, Stuart Battersby, Deb Suelzle, and Barbara Westlake.

About the Author

Kelli Houston is an award-winning healthcare executive, social justice advocate, and comedian with nearly two decades of experience in health and human services. She has led major Diversity, Equity, Inclusion, and Health Equity initiatives across organizations including Seattle Children's Hospital and Kaiser Permanente. She continues to lead diversity and equity work for healthcare systems. Born in Reno, Nevada, she now lives in the beautiful Pacific Northwest. Kelli holds an MBA and a Women in Leadership certification from Cornell University.

Speaker Page

Make an impact at your next conference by hiring Kelli Houston as your keynote speaker.

Houston is a community activist working on the ground floor of several projects in the service of her communities. She speaks from the heart about her life experiences being a gay woman of color and what we can do together as a community to help uplift each other.

To find out more, contact the author at khouston5057@gmail.com.

Book Club Questions

1. What were your takeaways from this memoir? What were the lasting impressions that kept you thinking after reading this?
2. What story stood out to you the most? Why?
3. Some themes around my life have revolved around fear. What was I afraid of? How much did that fear leave a lasting impact on my life?
4. What things are you afraid of? How might you work to push past those fears?
5. Throughout my life, I've struggled to find a place in many different jobs over the years. How has that impacted my sense of belonging?
6. Think about your own experiences. Where do you feel like you fit in the most, and why?
7. In a lot of positions I've been in I was the only Black, gay woman. Figuring out how to maneuver through those positions has helped me get to this point. How might you leverage your own differences to create a more welcoming environment for everyone?

8. Relationships are a big part of my story. That includes the relationships I've had with friends, partners, and my family, but more importantly the relationship with myself. How often do you see me overexerting myself for other people in my story? What lessons can you learn from those moments?
9. Think about your own relationships. What are some of the most impactful relationships you've had, either positive or negative?

Back of the Book Description

Kelli Houston's life began under a cloud of uncertainty, with her survival in question from the start. Her family viewed her as a miracle, strengthened by her grandmother's fervent prayers. This extraordinary status marked the start of a demanding path toward understanding herself.

From a young age, Kelli wrestled with her place within her family and among her peers. When she discovered a group where she felt accepted, she also recognized a profound difference within herself, a secret she shared with only a trusted few.

This memoir looks back at Kelli's childhood in the 1980s, when she was forced to conceal her identity as a lesbian. Hiding this part of herself shaped her friendships, creating some of her closest bonds while also creating distance between her and her family.

Kelli's narrative is infused with humor and candid honesty, offering a window into her personal world. Her story includes moments as a stand-up comedian and as an advocate for equity and justice. Through emotional struggles and difficult decisions in the pursuit of happiness, love, and redemption, Kelli discovered the importance of healing and self-worth.

The Unintentional Comedian is an inspiration for anyone who has felt out of place. With warmth and candor, she invites readers to celebrate authenticity and embrace the ongoing quest toward becoming their truest selves.

The B Corp Movement

Dear reader,

Thank you for reading this book and joining the Publish Your Purpose community! You are joining a special group of people who aim to make the world a better place.

What's Publish Your Purpose About?

Our mission is to elevate the voices often excluded from traditional publishing. We intentionally seek out authors and storytellers with diverse backgrounds, life experiences, and unique perspectives to publish books that will make an impact in the world.

Beyond our books, we are focused on tangible, action-based change. As a woman- and LGBTQ+-owned company, we are committed to reducing inequality, lowering levels of poverty, creating a healthier environment, building stronger communities, and creating high-quality jobs with dignity and purpose.

As a Certified B Corporation, we use business as a force for good. We join a community of mission-driven companies building a more equitable, inclusive, and sustainable global economy. B Corporations must meet high standards of transparency, social and environmental performance, and accountability as determined by the nonprofit B Lab. The certification process is rigorous and ongoing (with a recertification requirement every three years).

How Do We Do This?

We intentionally partner with socially and economically disadvantaged businesses that meet our sustainability goals. We embrace and encourage our authors and employee's differences in race, age, color, disability, ethnicity, family or marital status, gender identity or expression, language, national origin, physical and mental ability, political affiliation, religion, sexual orientation, socio-economic status, veteran status, and other characteristics that make them unique.

Community is at the heart of everything we do—from our writing and publishing programs to contributing to social enterprise nonprofits like reSET (https://www.resetco.org/) and our work in founding B Local Connecticut.

We are endlessly grateful to our authors, readers, and local community for being the driving force behind the equitable and sustainable world we are building together.

To connect with us online, or publish with us,
visit us at www.publishyourpurpose.com.

Elevating Your Voice,

Jenn T. Grace

Founder, Publish Your Purpose

www.ingramcontent.com/pod-product-compliance
Ingram Content Group UK Ltd.
Pitfield, Milton Keynes, MK11 3LW, UK
UKHW021905190726
13853UKWH00002B/512